THE TASK FORCE FOR CHILD SURVIVAL

The

TASK FORCE
for
CHILD
SURVIVAL

SECRETS OF
SUCCESSFUL COALITIONS

WILLIAM H. FOEGE
Foreword by **PRESIDENT JIMMY CARTER**

Johns Hopkins University Press | *Baltimore*

© 2018 Johns Hopkins University Press
All rights reserved. Published 2018.
Printed in the United States of America on acid-free paper
9 8 7 6 5 4 3 2 1

Johns Hopkins University Press
2715 North Charles Street
Baltimore, Maryland 21218-4363
www.press.jhu.edu

Library of Congress Cataloging-in-Publication Data

Names: Foege, William H., 1936– author.
Title: The Task Force for Child Survival : secrets of successful coalitions / William H.
  Foege ; foreword by President Jimmy Carter.
Description: Baltimore : Johns Hopkins University Press, 2018. | Includes
  bibliographical references and index.
Identifiers: LCCN 2017051886 | ISBN 9781421425603 (paperback : alk. paper) |
  ISBN 1421425602 (paperback : alk. paper) | ISBN 9781421425610 (electronic)
  | ISBN 1421425610 (electronic)
Subjects: | MESH: Emory University. Task Force for Child Survival. | Immunization
  Programs—history | Infant | Child | International Agencies—history | International
  Cooperation—history | Public Health Administration—history | History, 20th Century
Classification: LCC RA638 | NLM WS 11.1 | DDC 614.4/7083-dc23
  LC record available at https://lccn.loc.gov/2017051886

A catalog record for this book is available from the British Library.

Special discounts are available for bulk purchases of this book. For more information,
please contact Special Sales at 410-516-6936 or specialsales@press.jhu.edu.

Johns Hopkins University Press uses environmentally friendly book materials,
including recycled text paper that is composed of at least 30 percent post-consumer
waste, whenever possible.

To Carol Walters and in memory of William C. Watson Jr.

CONTENTS

FOREWORD

I am fortunate to have witnessed so much history, close up, over ninety-two years. One series of events is of special importance because I was allowed to participate: the improvements in health experienced by people around the world. With little fanfare, one disease, smallpox, has disappeared, and two, Guinea worm and polio, are about to exit. The deaths of children under age five have decreased by two-thirds—from 50,000 a day to 15,000 a day. AIDS has gone from a death sentence to a chronic disease. New vaccines will make diseases that once shortened life but footnotes in medical literature. Even poverty is declining globally, and a rational health future is possible.

This book describes some unusual events involved in this improvement. The first is an outside agency, the not-for-profit Task Force for Child Survival, formed in March 1984 to facilitate the work of huge global agencies. The heroes are Jim Grant, head of UNICEF, and Halfdan Mahler, head of the World Health Organization. Together with the World Bank, the UNDP (the United Nations Development Programme), and the Rockefeller Foundation, they recognized that turf wars between agencies were holding back immunization coverage in poor countries. These five organizations agreed to experiment with a small, outside private group to help them, and it worked. Within six years, immunization coverage increased from about 25 percent of children (depending on which vaccine was measured) to the announcement by Jim Grant at the Summit for Children on September 30, 1990, that 80 percent of children in the world had received at least one vaccine. Grant called it the greatest peacetime effort the world had ever seen.

I was pleased that I had nominated Jim to head UNICEF and was proud to have been involved in the global immunization effort, even to the point of administering polio vaccine to children during an immunization campaign in Colombia.

Another unusual development was the request by Merck & Co. to the Task Force to organize a distribution program for Mectizan, a drug that can prevent blindness caused by the parasite *Onchocerca volvulus*, which is spread by the bite of a black fly. In some parts of Africa, the majority of people in certain villages were blind by middle age or old age, before 1990. The Task Force chaired the Mectizan distribution program for Merck, and the Carter Center became the largest distributor of the medicine. So now there is even talk of eradicating *that* disease, river blindness. I was inspired when African heads of state agreed to make this disease a priority, and I visited Africa with Dr. Roy Vagelos, the CEO of Merck and the person who made the decision to distribute the drug without charge.

Thanks to the Bill & Melinda Gates Foundation, the global immunization program is flourishing: new vaccines are being distributed to poor countries, and coverage continues to improve for all vaccines. The example of Merck, which has now distributed over 1 billion doses of Mectizan at no cost, has inspired other companies to subsidize a variety of programs. The Task Force for Child Survival continues today as the Task Force for Global Health, one of the most effective nongovernmental organizations in the country.

This book tells the story of miracles in global health.

President Jimmy Carter

THE TASK FORCE FOR CHILD SURVIVAL

INTRODUCTION

There were early clues that global health might become a passion. My parents were interested in other countries, and my uncle and his family were missionaries in New Guinea in the 1930s. However, the real beginning was over sixty-six years ago, when I was fifteen years old.

We had no television, but we did not lack for entertainment. The Selkirk Mountain range in northeast Washington State provided opportunities for hiking, fishing, and swimming. Five siblings provided endless distractions, and at age fifteen, I had a variety of work experiences behind me, including having a newspaper route for three years and working in a service station and at drug stores in two different towns.

It was a surprise to have this busy life interrupted when I was encased in a body cast for three months at the age of fifteen to treat a separation of the head of my femur. I was unable to turn over, stand up, or change positions. To avoid isolation from key activities, my parents moved my bed into the living room, and our local doctor came to the house to apply the body cast.

One positive outcome was the opportunity to spend long hours reading, interrupted periodically by listening to the news on the radio. Both activities required imagination to translate what was written and heard into a mental image. My imagination was especially stirred by reading the book *Out of My Life and Thought* by Albert Schweitzer. He recounted a privileged upbringing, in which he spent years developing his passions, leading to three earned doctoral degrees—in theology, philosophy, and music. He became an accomplished organist and the world's authority on Bach and on organ building. But, at age thirty, he entered medical school and devoted the rest of his life to using his medical skills in Africa. The idea of medicine and Africa became a recurring thought of mine.

When Johns Hopkins University Press reprinted some of Schweitzer's books, his daughter, Rhena Schweitzer Miller, asked me to write a new foreword for *The Primeval Forest*. It gave me an opportunity, fifty years after my first reading, to rediscover the power of his example.

In medical school, finding people interested in global health was not an easy task. An exception was Rei Ravenholt, an epidemiologist and public health teacher. As the epidemiologist for the Seattle/King County Health Department, he also employed me after school and on Saturdays on research projects involving public health. He was well aware of the lack of career tracks in global health and said if I were truly interested, I should join the Epidemic Intelligence Service (EIS) at the Communicable Disease Center (CDC; now the Centers for Disease Control and Prevention) in Atlanta, Georgia. He advised that I would meet people interested in global health there and would make lifelong contacts. And he offered to write a letter of recommendation. He was correct; it was the perfect pathway.

My two years with the EIS led to two global health experiences. The first was to India in 1962 as a substitute Peace Corps physician, when that organization was recruiting to replace a physician who had become ill. The second was to Tonga, in 1963, as part of a group testing a foot-powered jet injector to determine the dilution of smallpox vaccine most appropriate for mass vaccination. Little did I know that I would be using that instrument in West Africa within a few years.

Mentors continued to be the fuel for my career. After Ravenholt, there was Alex Langmuir, the legendary epidemiologist at the CDC who created the EIS, and then Nobel laureate Tom Weller, my teacher for a year at the Harvard Tropical Public Health Program. Two years in Nigeria for both a church group and the CDC allowed us to develop a more efficient approach to smallpox eradication, wherein we abandoned mass vaccination, concentrating instead on finding the virus and identifying and protecting those at immediate risk of the disease (1).

In 1970, I had the opportunity to become head of the smallpox program at the CDC and assigned myself to India in 1973. By May 1974, we had even perfected surveillance/containment approaches for highly smallpox-endemic areas, and India went from exceedingly high rates of smallpox in that same month to zero cases in the entire country twelve months later. The country recorded its last case in May 1975.

I had the opportunity to become director of the CDC in early 1977, a challenging and exceedingly exciting position. The eradication of smallpox in the entire world was announced in early 1980, and global health received increasing attention.

In 1984, with the help of Halfdan Mahler, head of the World Health Organization (WHO), and Jim Grant, head of UNICEF, a Task Force was formed to attempt to improve global immunization coverage. That is the subject of this book.

The success in increasing immunization levels around the world in six years' time whetted my appetite for more global health work. At the request of Merck, I chaired the Mectizan Expert Committee for twelve years in its very successful donation program to counter river blindness. As with smallpox, a disease called onchocerciasis, which left many people blind in certain areas of Africa, went, in a single generation, from a constant worry for those who were exposed, to a nonexistent condition known only by history.

Working as executive director of the Carter Center opened up new vistas as I saw how influential President and Mrs. Rosalynn Carter were at using political skills in promoting global health.

As a professor of international health at Emory University, I saw an increased interest in the field of global health that had simply not existed when I was in school. This interest was supported by the Hubert family of Atlanta, Georgia, who provided significant resources for global health activities at both Emory University and Duke University.

Finally, work with the Bill & Melinda Gates Foundation, from 1999 to 2011, allowed me to see the blossoming of a new age in global health. There are now more resources, more political support, and a large cohort of students interested in global health equity.

These varied experiences forced me to look back at the very unorthodox attempt, in 1984, to leverage change in the largest of global health agencies with a small, independent task force actually supported by those same agencies. In retrospect, it is still a miracle, lost to history unless it is told from various perspectives. This is my perspective.

chapter 1

THE PLOT

On March 13, 1984, thirty-four people gathered at the invitation of the Rockefeller Foundation at its center in Bellagio, Italy, to plan an acceleration of the global immunization campaign. By September 1990, the objective of that meeting had been met: 80 percent of the children in the world had received at least one vaccine. It was the "largest peacetime achievement the world had ever seen," declared Jim Grant, executive director of UNICEF, at the Summit for Children that year.

Behind the scenes of these events was a little-known facilitator, the Task Force for Child Survival. It consisted initially of just three people, who parlayed their commitment to global health equity into a worldwide force led by five giants in that world: the Rockefeller Foundation, UNICEF, the WHO, the United Nations Development Programme, and the World Bank.

The intent had been to disband the Task Force after 1990, but it had proved to be too useful to abandon. Thirty years later, three programs, spawned in various ways by that meeting, remain, each one a multi-billion-dollar contribution to global health. Just one of these, for example, Merck & Co.'s Mectizan Donation Program for onchocerciasis, has donated more than 1 billion treatments to prevent river blindness. And it did this with no global superstructure by following the Task Force model, with a coalition held together solely by an expert committee and a shared objective.

In 2013, the *Chronicle of Philanthropy* listed the Task Force as the fourth most successful organization in the nation in its ability to raise resources (1).

So how did this happen? How did a small, informal group of three former CDC professionals end up being a vital, yet almost anonymous, part of such a history? Well, for one thing, attributes like *small, informal,* and *anonymous* were not accidental but, rather, assets in this process. This is the story of the Task Force for Child Survival. It is also the story of how successful coalitions happen.

chapter 2

IMMUNIZATIONS IN THE UNITED STATES

When I was born in 1936, my baby book indicates I received only two vaccines—smallpox and diphtheria toxoid. When I became interested in global health in the mid-twentieth century, few vaccines were routinely used. The smallpox vaccine was standard; BCG (Bacille Calmette Guerin vaccine) was given to prevent tuberculosis; and a combination vaccine, which contained pertussis bacterial vaccine and two toxoid vaccines for tetanus and diphtheria, was used.

The real breakthrough was the announcement of the polio vaccine at a University of Michigan press conference in April 1955. Tommy Francis Jr., a virologist, had just concluded a field trial involving 1.8 million children. He entered the packed auditorium and summed up his following announcement in four words: "Safe, effective, and potent." That inaugurated a new era in vaccine science.

It also initiated a new era in social equity. The day after Francis's announcement, there was spontaneous rejoicing around the country. But the public could not believe no government plan existed for administering the polio vaccine. So President Dwight D. Eisenhower ordered Oveta Culp Hobby, the secretary of Health, Education and Welfare (HEW), to develop a plan.

When Mrs. Hobby had arrived in Washington, DC, she was opposed to anything that resembled socialized medicine. But following the president's order and the nation's fervor for the polio vaccine, she held a press conference to say she would seek an appropriation to buy vaccine for poor children. Senator Lister Hill then held a press conference to say, in effect, that no American children should have to declare themselves poor to receive the vaccine, and he would seek an appropriation to purchase polio vaccine for *all* the children in the country. This was the day that vaccines became both a personal good *and* a social good. The era of equity in vaccine coverage had begun.

Ten years later, President Lyndon Johnson used the same reasoning to commit the United States to social equity through the attempt to eradicate smallpox.

A decade after the smallpox program began, the World Health Assembly practiced social equity by starting the Expanded Programme on Immunization to provide immunizations for all children of the world.

In the early 1960s, the measles vaccine became available. Until that point, the measles virus had been the most lethal agent in the world, causing more than 3 million deaths a year. And then the production of new vaccines proliferated, with microbiologist Maurice Hilleman becoming the Louis Pasteur of modern times. Eventually, Hilleman became even greater than Pasteur: more than half the vaccines given to children around the world emanated from his mind. Because he worked for the pharmaceutical company Merck & Co., he never achieved the scientific and public acclaim that he deserved. Plus, he was a modest man, who did not put his name on any of his vaccines. The closest he came was to name the Jeryl Lynn vaccine strain of the mumps vaccine after his daughter. While she was ill, he isolated the virus from her and used that isolate to develop the vaccine.

During the 1960s and 1970s, the Centers for Disease Control (CDC*) worked with states to develop childhood immunization programs. Two governors' wives were active in establishing state pro-

*This was its name at that time. Since then, the CDC acronym has been kept, but the official name of the agency has changed, at present, to the Centers for Disease Control and Prevention.

grams, Rosalynn Carter in Georgia and Betty Bumpers in Arkansas. After President Jimmy Carter was inaugurated in 1977, the Carters invited Senator and Mrs. Bumpers to the White House for dinner and discussed opportunities to improve the immunization status of children in the United States. The next day the president called Joseph Califano, the new secretary of HEW, to discuss what could be done quickly to improve immunization programs. Califano called me, as director of the CDC, and asked whether we could set a target of reaching 90 percent of children by the time they entered school. I, in turn, discussed the target with J. D. Millar, the CDC physician who headed the national immunization program. He told me that to date no program had achieved that level of coverage, and he would hate to see such a target in his job description. But on reflection, he agreed. The next day it was in his job description.

The immunization program operators soon reported that the states with an immunization requirement for school entry had the best results and suggested such a goal should be sought in all states. With experience, it was found that higher levels, even exceeding 95 percent coverage, could be achieved by setting mandatory school-entry requirements.

But it was also discovered that school age was too late for optimal results. Indeed, coverage by age two years was required for maximum impact. Characteristically, and with great energy, Mrs. Carter and Mrs. Bumpers formed a group called Every Child by Two to get political leaders, health leaders, educators, church leaders, and others to promote early immunization.

Disease rates for vaccine-preventable diseases plummeted, and success begat success. Eventually, these successes led to discussions about the feasibility of interrupting measles transmission in the country.

Measles is incredibly contagious. The virus seeks out susceptible persons with laser-like accuracy and tenacity. Introduce a case of smallpox to a classroom with susceptible children and perhaps a third will acquire smallpox in the next incubation period. Do the same with a case of measles and 80 percent of the children will have measles one incubation period later. Many experts thought interrupting measles transmission was not possible and that to even state that as a goal could harm the CDC's reputation. Nevertheless, we finally decided that the ultimate barriers to interrupting transmission would not be known unless we selected the ultimate objective.

An intense effort was launched to determine whether the chain of measles transmission could be broken. As the CDC director, I met for thirty minutes each week with members of the immunization program to review, summarize, and strategize the nation's measles goals. The initial barriers were easily identified and solved. Military recruits were spreading measles after basic training when they went home on furlough. When the military changed its procedures to immunize every new recruit, regardless of a history of measles disease or measles vaccinations, the spread stopped.

The next identified problem was that the measles virus was spreading through preschools. So states changed laws to require immunization for entrance to preschool. Measles virus was also found to spread through colleges and universities. Consequently, states and institutions of higher learning changed their entrance requirements. One by one, the barriers were identified and removed.

The ultimate barrier—imported measles cases—had been hidden among the other reasons for measles spread. The United States was experiencing an average of two importations of measles a week from other countries, which had escaped detection because transmission had been occurring from so many other sources. The Pan American Health Organization launched an effort to eliminate measles from the hemisphere, and importations were reduced. By the mid-1980s, we registered the first week without a reported case of measles.

So, by 1983, protection of children in the United States from vaccine-preventable diseases had reached a high level of perfection. And systems were in place to protect every child as new vaccines were quickly becoming available.

In 2012, the American Red Cross held a meeting to review measles in the world. A coalition of groups had given 1 billion measles injections in the previous ten years, and global eradication was discussed as a feasible goal. Some felt that polio needed to be eradicated first, lest attention to measles detract from funding for polio. Others felt no concern about two eradication programs being conducted simultaneously.

Ironically, the highly contagious nature of measles turned out to be a key factor in eradication rather than an obstacle. Measles is readily recognized clinically—unlike polio, which may require 100 to 1,000 infected people before a clinical case is obvious. The rapid spread may make measles outbreaks obvious so that an affected area can be quickly saturated with vaccinators to halt the spread of infection. Chain after chain of transmission could thus be interrupted until the last chain is removed and the world would be declared measles-free.

In 2017, the debate continues. Could the eradication of measles actually happen?

chapter 3

PROTECTING THE WORLD'S CHILDREN

The first tool in the public health toolbox was the smallpox vaccine, first used by Edward Jenner in 1796. The field was agonizingly slow to develop, however. So 140 years later, when I was born, only diphtheria toxoid had been added to smallpox for routine use. But then the field accelerated.

Now two dozen vaccines are routinely used in various parts of the world. And for good reason. Vaccines provide a key foundation for global health. Pathogens mutate to accommodate to antibiotics; this mutation does not occur with vaccines. To date, vaccines have remained stable in their ability to provide long-term immunity and require limited visits to a vaccinator. Some viruses, such as influenza, are able to recombine antigens in an attempt to fool the immune system, but even they have a relatively small number of antigens that they use. At some point, we will likely have flu vaccines that include all known influenza antigens. Unlike antibiotics, vaccines usually do not have to be repeated with each illness, and they often provide lifetime protection.

Success in Eradicating Smallpox

As the Carter administration strengthened the domestic immunization program, a major push was under way at the World Health Organization (WHO) to provide vaccines for all the children of the world. The world had just completed a decadelong program to eradicate smallpox. The WHO estimated that 300 million people had died of smallpox in the twentieth century, and in 1965 and 1966, the World Health Assembly adopted resolutions and then a budget to eliminate the disease in ten years.

The WHO demonstrated that it was possible to select a global objective, organize to achieve that objective, develop strategies and assessment tools, make midcourse corrections, and free the world of an age-old scourge. As David Sencer, director of the CDC until 1976, said, smallpox eradication increased the confidence of the public health workforce of the world to realize what they could do and then to eagerly seek new objectives to improve health. Smallpox eradication had given the WHO new courage, and the use of other vaccines seemed a reasonable next step.

The Next Steps

In May 1974, the World Health Assembly passed a resolution to support an Expanded Programme on Immunization (EPI), which would use some of the techniques, staff, and systems developed by the smallpox program. Without the success of smallpox, such a resolution could not have been imagined. In the fall of 1976, physician Ralph (Rafe) Henderson, one of the smallpox eradication pioneers, was recruited to head the program. He was in place at the WHO's headquarters in Geneva in early 1977. This was about the time President Carter made his call to Secretary Califano, requesting an emphasis on immunization in the United States.

The WHO estimated that less than 5 percent of children in the developing world were receiving vaccines; even the traditional vaccines, such as DPT (diphtheria, pertussis, tetanus), were reaching only a small percentage of children. The vaccine with the highest coverage was BCG, a vaccine given to prevent tuberculosis, and the irony is that it was marginally useful in preventing disease. The challenges for improvement were huge. But so were the opportunities.

Rafe Henderson was an inspired choice to head up this new program. With a medical degree, a public health degree, and a Master of Public Policy degree from the Kennedy School at Harvard, plus experience in West Africa's smallpox eradication program, he brought the credentials but also the right persona. He spoke French and was low key and affable in his approach to people, but he had an absolute intensity when pursuing an objective that he desired. An advantage not shared by many people at the WHO was that he had wrestled through the problems of heat, humidity, lost supplies, and rural challenges while working in Africa.

Henderson's other advantage was CDC sponsorship. Some years earlier, Dave Sencer had asked me to chair a small group to advise him on how the CDC could best improve global health. At that time, the US Congress was very parochial and believed the CDC's mission was solely to improve the health of Americans. Congress often failed to see that global health is all inclusive and can't be separated into domestic versus foreign realms. Our advice to Sencer was to put some of the best CDC managers, at the CDC's expense, into positions where global health decisions were being made, with the WHO Geneva as the first place to explore. Sencer had followed that advice with a number of assignees, and Rafe Henderson was one of them.

The WHO's restraints are real. The WHO must have some national balance in those it hires. Many of those on the payroll can't afford to lose their jobs, and therefore must always make conservative decisions. However, governments' sponsorship of employees, as long as the WHO could make the decisions on whether to accept the employees, would allow for ones more likely to make courageous and principled decisions because they would have an organization to which they could return. But it is essential that the sponsoring country give up all supervisory rights while that person is in a WHO position. Henderson could and did make courageous decisions.

Architects of Cold-Chain Technology

Henderson recruited people who had proved their abilities in the smallpox eradication program and set to work doing the basics. Keeping vaccine cold from production to injection (i.e., the cold chain) may seem straightforward, but it is an enormous task. At so many points along the supply chain, vaccine can be left unrefrigerated long enough to lose potency. One could not be sure that refrigerated vaccine in a health center was actually potent. One of the most discouraging times for an immunization supervisor was to make an unannounced visit to a health center and find the vaccine on a shelf and the refrigerator being used for cooling beer. There was no way to tell good vaccine from bad vaccine until children later developed measles or pertussis.

With two dedicated workers at the WHO, John Lloyd and James Cheyne, equipment and systems were developed to improve the cold chain. The 3M Company, together with the Seattle-based Program for Appropriate Technology in Health, a nongovernmental agency (NGO), developed a temperature-sensitive card to be placed in each carton of vaccine and later a small marker to be placed on each vial of vaccine that would change color with time and temperature when heated. (High temperatures over a short period ruin the vaccine. Marginal temperatures take much longer. The color change is calibrated to the endpoint of impotent vaccine.) These advances along with an operations manual, prepared by Dr. Ko Keja and others, began the development of systems that could be used for training programs around the world. Dr. Keja, from the Netherlands, was the prototype for a global health worker—smart, indefatigable, optimistic, field oriented, and likable.

One of the most discouraging times for an immunization supervisor was to make an unannounced visit to a health center and find the vaccine on a shelf and the refrigerator being used for cooling beer.

But it was labor intensive to initiate and support programs in dozens of countries. Headquarters was always overwhelmed.

In theory, everything should fall into place. As the WHO developed standards for vaccine development, needles and syringes, systems to be used, methods of immunizing, evaluation techniques, and the like, it provided a blueprint for immunization. It should then be possible for ministries of health, NGOs, and UNICEF to acquire the correct supplies and conduct immunization programs using the WHO standards and procedures.

Jealousy over Turf

But the foibles of people can lead to jealousy over turf, concern over who is listened to, or the need to advertise one's organization to acquire resources. Even the heads of international agencies are not immune, especially when they become entangled in arguments on horizontal programs (improving infrastructure capacity) versus vertical programs (emphasizing specific programs, such as immunization or oral rehydration). The arguments can be traced back at least 130 years and continue to this day.

In 1978, the WHO and UNICEF, with the help of the Soviet government, helped sponsor a program in Alma-Ata to promote primary health care. The group defined eight essentials in primary health care, including health education, safe water, immunization, and the provision of essential drugs. As the EPI enlarged, the director of the WHO, Dr. Halfdan Mahler, was intent on promoting primary health care in general as the program's strength. He understood the need for passionate individuals to concentrate on specific aspects, such as immunization, but he was determined to promote primary health care, with immunization contributing to the whole rather than to a vertical program.

UNICEF, however, wanted to define the highest priorities in the health needs of children and concentrate on a small number of priorities that could be accomplished in the near future. Jim Grant, who had become director of UNICEF in 1980 on the recommendation of President Carter, was in perpetual motion from the first. After briefings from a large number of people, he had decided on four priorities for UNICEF—growth monitoring, oral rehydration, breastfeeding, and immunization, or GOBI.

A Personal Perspective

In 1986, as president of the American Public Health Association (APHA), I was to give a keynote talk at the annual convention. I admire this organization because its lobbying efforts are always concentrated on improving the health of the public rather than on improving the lot of public health workers. So I was proud to be involved.

In the process of preparing for my talk, I became curious about APHA's meeting 100 years earlier, so I went to the 1886 archives. To my great surprise, I found that participants at *that* meeting had also been discussing horizontal versus vertical approaches to improving health. I had thought it was a recent argument, limited to the global health community.

I realized we had a century of experience to draw from and asked myself what had actually happened in the United States regarding this argument. It seemed clear that every time public health had a tool we attempted to exploit it. This, in turn, improved the capacity to address the use of the next tool. So public health in the United States was historically a balancing act, alternating vertical programs that improved infrastructure, followed by horizontal growth, which aided the next vertical approach.

Infrastructure without a tool is meaningless, while a tool without infrastructure goes unused. Balance of the two approaches is the answer rather than one or the other. I stopped engaging in such arguments as a nonproductive use of time, but they still consumed valuable time and resources at almost every global health meeting.

Although oral rehydration had captured Grant's early attention because it did not require a cold chain and a large delivery program, he made immunization a top priority after a briefing by Rafe Henderson and exposure to such a program in Colombia, which demonstrated improved immunization rates when all sectors of society mobilized for special immunization days.

The problem was that this selection of priorities did not fit well with the WHO's desire for a balanced approach to primary health care. Mahler felt undermined, and he referred to this in his talk to the World Health Assembly in 1983. He called such initiatives "red herrings." The global health world realized whom this comment was aimed at and that it was, in effect, a shot across the bow, a warning from the WHO to UNICEF. But Jim Grant was not vindictive and therefore did not respond in kind. He also did not change his approach, and UNICEF persisted in its new strategy.

chapter 4

HOW PRODUCTIVE COALITIONS BEGIN

Various "vectors" came together in the early 1980s to cause "disease" in the global health community. It was not just competition between the global agencies and continuous arguments over vertical versus horizontal approaches. Bilateral agencies* were also growing in influence and wanted to be involved in immunization programs because the results are so tangible.

Many countries formed bilateral agencies after World War II to provide health, agricultural, and development assistance to poor countries. Although these agencies were based on a desire to assist as well as, perhaps, a need to advance national pride and extend influence, a spectrum of approaches evolved. Some, such as the Swedish International Development Agency, developed a reputation for sensitive emphasis on the needs of recipient countries. Others, such as the US Agency for International Development, were often considered, rightly or wrongly, to be blunt instruments of political power. These agencies greatly helped resource-poor countries, but they extracted a price. They often became competitive at the country level

*Bilateral refers to a government agency or nonprofit organization that is based in a single country but provides aid, including medical aid or disaster relief, for people in other countries.

and required the time of finance and health ministries, already short of time and personnel, to negotiate simultaneously with multiple agencies.

UNICEF and the WHO were both driving hard for improved delivery of vaccines. But they had an additional challenge: new vaccines were on the horizon. It was essential to improve the delivery system for currently available vaccines but also to keep in mind the need to deliver even more vaccines in the future.

The WHO program let everyone know it was ready. It had an infrastructure, and it could build a global program if it could acquire the resources.

Then Jonas Salk entered the arena. He wanted the inactivated polio vaccine to be used in the global program. His was a persuasive voice. He had the support of vaccine leaders in France. Together, Salk and French researchers conducted studies in Africa to demonstrate that a two-dose schedule of Salk inactivated vaccine (IPV) would be sufficient to stop polio in Africa. As Salk was completing those studies—well, let Rafe Henderson take up the story from his recent memoir:

> By 1982, with preliminary results from these studies in hand, Salk approached Dr. Ken Warren, Director of the Health Sciences Division of the Rockefeller Foundation, to promote his idea. Ken approached Jim Grant and they approached Robert McNamara, President of the World Bank. So far, so good. But McNamara insisted that WHO also be included. That was not good news for Salk!
>
> McNamara was convinced that the donor community would contribute an additional $100 million per year to support immunization in developing countries and it was decided that a meeting of donors, jointly sponsored by the Rockefeller Foundation, the World Bank, WHO, UNICEF and UNDP [United Nations Development Programme], would be convened in March 1984 at the Rockefeller facilities in Bellagio, Italy. (1)

There were others who saw the excellent US immunization program and asked how to replicate it in developing areas of the world. The answer started with figuring out how to assist the WHO and

An Ongoing Debate

The IPV (inactivated polio vaccine) versus OPV (oral polio vaccine) controversy is too complex to fully describe in this book. So, instead, I will provide my short and biased view. In the United States, IPV was first used because it was the first developed. Polio incidence decreased rapidly after the introduction of IPV (Salk vaccine) in 1955. It provided protection from poliovirus, which multiplies in the intestine, from moving to the central nervous system and causing paralysis. OPV (Sabin) multiplies in the intestine and protects against wild poliovirus's multiplying in the future in the intestine. OPV also protects against wild virus going to the central nervous system and causing paralysis. The vaccine virus can spread to other children, in the same way the wild virus would, providing protection to children even beyond the group actually vaccinated.

The debate was settled in favor of OPV because of the ease of administration (oral) and the advantage of intestinal immunity, which limits wild virus multiplication if wild polioviruses are encountered in the future.

The arguments are basically valid. What was not totally under-stood at the time was that even IPV reduced intestinal virus multipli-cation on exposure to wild virus and that OPV had lowered efficacy in tropical (as opposed to temperate) climates. In tropical areas, especially in areas of high population density, competing viruses reduced the effectiveness of OPV. CDC-conducted studies in Africa showed the need for multiple doses of oral vaccine to get more than 90 percent protection—indeed, as many as ten doses for 95 percent protection against type 3 poliovirus. The use of both IPV and OPV in the same child enhanced protection with fewer doses of vaccine. The major cost of immunization programs involves reaching a child. The cost increases when four, five, six, or more visits are required.

A better solution would have been to use OPV as planned, adding IPV to the DPT vaccine, which would not have required extra sy-ringes, needles, or vaccinators. It would have been a hidden benefit except for the cost of the IPV vaccine itself. That cost could have been very high and still have been cost-beneficial if it had saved one or more vaccinator visits to a child.

In essence, the program started with one hand tied behind the back of the polio eradicators rather than using all the tools available. A midcourse correction became very difficult for the WHO, and those advising the WHO, to adopt. Therefore, the WHO hesitated for years, and then decades, to make such a reasonable change in strategy.

UNICEF to improve their immunization programs, how to improve their ability to work together, and how to increase resources available.

Ego Suppression

A strange thing happened as plans were devised for the initial meeting of donors to accelerate the global immunization campaign, to be held at the Rockefeller Center in Bellagio, Italy. Jim Grant and Halfdan Mahler met privately with me, and for a short time, I felt like a therapist. They told me that they both had such big egos that they sometimes had trouble getting along. They said, "No wonder our agencies have trouble working with each other." But they both knew that for the good of child health they had to figure out a way to make immunization programs work.

They said they had no idea how the Bellagio meeting would go, but if a task force were to be put together to facilitate child health and global immunization, would I agree to be in charge? Here is the first lesson in building productive coalitions: one needs the total commitment and support of the top people of the agencies involved. Even the best ideas are likely to be unused if they do not have the support of the agency leaders.

The second lesson for coalitions is that one must identify the final mile—the ultimate goal. Agreeing to work together because of similar interests (in this case child health and immunizations in particular) is not enough. One must define the last mile in a way that people know what they are agreeing to do. In this case, the WHO and UNICEF were interested in a program that could reach most children by 1990. (This was later defined as 80 percent coverage by that date.)

The third lesson in coalitions that work well is that one needs to practice ego suppression. Guarding turf, seeking credit, or becoming the spokesperson is hazardous to the health of the coalition. If I agreed to lead such a task force, Grant and Mahler said, we needed to understand in advance that it could never compete with the agencies, it must keep an appropriately low profile, and it should never use the word *coordinate* because neither agency wanted to be coordinated nor would any other agency that agreed to be part of the coalition. The word we settled on was *facilitate*. I was also asked to prepare ideas on the structure and function of such a task force to present at the Bellagio meeting

---

The first lesson in productive coalitions is that one needs the support of top people in the agencies involved.

I was about to leave the directorship of CDC. Because global health was my prime interest, I agreed to accept the challenge of heading up the task force if that were the decision of the Bellagio conference.

chapter 5
BELLAGIO, MARCH 1984

The behavior of mankind on the big stage is as surprising and fasci-
nating as anything biologists are discovering in subliminal genetics.
Who would think that something called The Task Force for Child
Survival . . . could be anything but a P.R. stunt? Surprise: not so. It was
indeed a rare conjuncture of circumstances and people that engendered
this lively hybrid where, for a decade, minds and hearts, institutions
and experts followed a common star: to save and protect all children
everywhere. —NEWTON BOWLES, *The Task Force for Child Survival and
Development—Hope as Energy*

It was an unusually influential group that met on March 13, 1984,
at the Rockefeller Center in Bellagio, Italy (1).* So unusual that it is
worth mentioning some of the attendees. In addition to the president of the Rockefeller Foundation, Richard Lyman, there were
Halfdan Mahler, director-general of the WHO; Jim Grant, executive
director of UNICEF; A. W. Clausen, president of the World Bank;
and Brad Morse, administrator of the United Nations Development
Programme (UNDP). Participants included Jonas Salk, developer of
the first polio vaccine, and Robert McNamara, former president of
the World Bank. Respected scientists and administrators included
Jan Kostrzewski of Poland, one of the most highly regarded scientists in Europe; V. Ramalingaswami, perhaps the most respected
scientist in India; Margaret Catley-Carlson, president of the Canadian International Development Agency, who has a reputation for
innovation and decisiveness; Mamadou Diop, minister of health in
Senegal; Gus Nossal, one of the world's leading vaccine researchers
from Australia; and Peter McPherson, administrator for US Agency
for International Development (USAID).

*The Rockefeller Foundation's contributions to public health are legend.
See appendix A.

CONFERENCE REPORT

WHO UNICEF World Bank UNDP RF

PROTECTING THE WORLD'S CHILDREN:
Vaccines and Immunization
within Primary Health Care

Cover of conference report from the first Bellagio conference, Bellagio, Italy, March 13-15, 1984. *Protecting the World's Children: Vaccines and Immunizations within Primary Health Care,* Conference Report (New York: The Rockefeller Foundation, 1984)

A contingent of people who had labored in the global health arena also attended, including D. A. Henderson, dean of the Johns Hopkins School of Hygiene and Public Health; Rafe Henderson, head of the WHO immunization program; Nyle Brady from USAID; Joshua Cohen from the WHO; Steve Joseph from UNICEF; Philippe Stoeckel from the Agence de la Médicine Préventive (AMP) in France; and Ken Warren from the Rockefeller Foundation. There were others,

The delegates to the first Bellagio conference, in March 1984. *Back row, left to right:* Steve Joseph (US), Jan Kostrzewski (Poland), John North (UK), T. P. Svennevig (Norway), Ken Warren (US), Sergio Cattani (Italy), D. A. Henderson (US), William Mashler (US), Gus Nossal (Australia), Joshua Cohen (Switzerland), Philippe Stoeckel (France), Peter McPherson (US). *Middle row, left to right:* Nyle Brady (US), Mady Oury Sylla (Senegal), Reuben Sternfeld (US), Wolfgang Albert (W. Germany), R. McGovern (Australia), R. S. Porter (UK), Margaret Catley-Carlson (Canada), Rafe Henderson (US), Anders Forsse (Sweden), William Foege (US), Mogens Isaksen (Denmark). *Front row, left to right:* V. Ramalingaswami (India), Halfdan Mahler (Denmark), Richard Lyman (US), A. W. Clausen (US), Brad Morse (US), Jim Grant (US), Mamadou Diop (Senegal), Jonas Salk (US), Robert McNamara (US). Not shown: M. C. Arango-Echavarria (Colombia). Photo by Christopher Warren

but this gives the picture of the unusually high-level group of decision makers and experienced field people at the meeting.

At the meeting, Rafe Henderson discussed the global vaccine-preventable disease burden. He presented a table showing the distribution of more than 4.3 million deaths per year from measles, tetanus, and pertussis alone (2). This high mortality rate was true even eight years after the WHO's Expanded Programme on Immunization had been initiated. He reported on the status of that program. Training programs now included thousands of workers around the world. Standards had been developed, vaccine procurement had been streamlined, information systems were improving, and evaluation mechanisms were emphasized. In those first eight years of the program, coverage rates had increased from less than 5 percent in the developing world to a level of approximately 30 percent for the third dose of DPT, 24 percent for a third dose of polio, and approximately 14 percent for measles. While this was strong progress, he emphasized that the program also required strong acceleration.

It was both encouraging to hear of such progress and discouraging to appreciate that more than 12,000 children were still dying on an average day from the three easily preventable diseases alone. He ended his presentation by emphasizing the need to strengthen primary health care through immunization but also pointed out that the infrastructure was so poor in many places that the absorptive capacity for even including immunization was limited.

Rafe Henderson then presented a paper on the state of the art for vaccines—the countries producing them; training and supervision of health workers; and monitoring, evaluation, and research developments. The positive news was that the vaccine cost to fully protect an infant against polio, measles, diphtheria, tetanus, and pertussis—including BCG and a booster—was about the cost of a latte today. An absolute bargain.

Gus Nossal presented an upbeat review of how the biotechnology revolution was about to provide additional vaccines for hepatitis, malaria, and diarrheal diseases. D. A. Henderson looked at how immunization programs could accelerate the development of primary health care and asked how we could use the techniques of merchandising and social marketing to expand primary health care. Philippe Stoeckel summarized the results of the AMP's African studies, which used a two-dose inactivated polio vaccine strategy.

I then presented a proposal for a Task Force for Child Survival, which might facilitate the acceleration of immunization programs. An analysis of eleven national programs suggested that about 80 percent of costs were provided by the national government, and only 20 percent came from external sources. This confirmed the interest of countries in supporting immunization programs and suggested such programs would become part of the national infrastructure.

The cost of vaccines accounted for only about 12 percent of total costs. The great majority of costs involved a system for actually reaching children to give them the vaccines. This required salaries and transportation for vaccinators, health educators, logistics experts, and evaluators; office support; sterilization equipment, interpreters, per diems, and the like. I then provided cost estimates for various coverage rates for the next fifteen years.

After the presentations, the entire meeting was devoted to discussion. Steve Joseph of UNICEF, acting as rapporteur, provided a summary at the end of the third day with the following conclusions.

Themes

Conference participants were optimistic about the state of the science related to vaccines, the cold chain, and the methods of administration. Attendees were also optimistic about the progress to date, opportunities, and the art of the possible. Counteracting this was a "somber" view, especially from bilateral agencies, that resources were not likely to be available, and skepticism, especially about Robert McNamara's assertion that $100 million of new money could change everything. Finally, there was a very realistic appraisal of what could be done, given the constraints.

The possibility of a task force being created to facilitate the various agency contributions was met with strong resistance from bilateral agencies opposed to a new institutional structure. Yet existing structures were not leading to rapid protection of children.

At the end, Jim Grant put forth a proposal for an ad hoc task force to be supported by the five agencies sponsoring the meeting (the Rockefeller Foundation, UNICEF, WHO, UNDP, and the World Bank). His proposal was that I would be engaged as a joint consultant to the WHO and UNICEF, with initial support from the Rockefeller Foundation.

Grant proposed three objectives. First, the task force would work with India, Senegal, and Colombia to explore ways to accelerate country programs. Second, the task force should identify operational and biotechnical research needs to foster acceleration. Third, it should prepare an agenda based on those findings to present at a second Bellagio meeting to be held in two years.

Despite the negative reaction of some, participants were moved by Grant's passion and agreed to his proposal. The meeting ended with high hopes.

The conference report expressed that optimism: "The outcome is a plan not only to immunize all of the world's children . . . but to promote other effective means . . . to reduce morbidity and mortality" (1).

chapter 6

ORGANIZING A TASK FORCE SECRETARIAT

To have agreement from the top policy makers in the world that immunization was a priority presented an opportunity that needed to be exploited. Now we had the challenge of organizing a task force secretariat, an agenda for future action, and a mechanism for implementing that agenda. On reflection years later, I can say that almost every step turned out better than any of us could have expected.

When I returned to Atlanta, in my last days as director of the CDC, I asked my deputy, William Watson, and my assistant, Carol Walters, if they were interested in joining this effort. They were. I then talked to Dr. Jim Mason, the person who would become the new head of the CDC. He had asked me to stay on to work on planning and evaluation, and I had agreed. I now asked whether the CDC would support me half-time to work on the Task Force for Child Survival. My reasoning was that it would give me direct access to CDC personnel and resources and it would reduce the budget needs of the new Task Force if my salary came from the CDC. He agreed, and we took the next steps.

Carol Walters had worked in the front office of the CDC for many years and knew how to get things accomplished in that organization. Her contacts would be invaluable in identifying people who could assist the Task Force.

Bill Watson had worked his way up the ranks from venereal disease investigator to deputy director of the CDC. He had demonstrated social skills in working with a wide variety of people. (One of his oft-repeated pieces of advice was, "There is never an excuse for bad manners.") He also had great management skills and loved the challenge of solving an impossible managerial problem.

We started informally but later formed a nonprofit organization (known in the United States as a 501(c)(3) organization); the three of us constituted the board. The small size of the board and the fact that we had worked together for years made it possible to make even major decisions on the fly, even on the way to lunch sometimes. Carol would later write the decisions up and we would approve.

A small, lean organization can't afford all of the specialists and skills required of larger organizations. So I next went to see the president of Emory University, Dr. Jim Laney. Laney had a broad view of the world and the role of a university. He had worked in Korea in the military and had returned on his own to that country later. After leaving the presidency of Emory University, he was named US ambassador to South Korea. He had also been dean of the School of Theology at Emory. He was wise, erudite, and down to earth.

- -
Global health requires optimism; it can't afford the time to deal with negative people.
- -

I reviewed the Bellagio meeting and our hopes for a small secretariat to facilitate improvements in immunization. I told him that we could scarcely divert resources to develop retirement plans, travel regulations, and the dozens of functions performed in departments of human resources in larger organizations. My question, Could we imbed a 501(c)(3) organization into the Emory structure and thereby rent all of the services needed? He saw this as a legitimate role for Emory and agreed. Then we discussed how much overhead should be paid for these services. He pointed out that overhead at universities tended to be quite high; often grants find half their resources absorbed in overhead. But to provide a valued service to the world, he proposed that we pay overhead of 8 percent. I could scarcely believe the largess of this proposal and accepted with alacrity so that he would not have time for second thoughts.

The final decision involved a reporting structure. Laney said there had to be a reporting line to accomplish setting up and administering all of these things and proposed that I report to the dean of the medical school. Laney did not know that I had interacted with the dean for many years before he arrived at Emory. Although he was very intelligent, he was the kind of person I had learned to avoid, as his first reaction to most things was negative. Global health requires optimism; it can't afford the time to deal with negative people. I didn't feel I could say that after everything Laney had just granted, so instead I said to him, "That might work fine but let me at least throw out one other proposal. What if I would report directly to you if I promise in advance that I will never bother you?" He looked surprised, reflected for a minute, and smiled as he said, "OK." He understood, as did I, that reporting directly to him would provide me access to all the people at Emory. While I did report on various occasions what was happening, I never did bother him.

We acquired office space near the CDC and began to plan for the next steps of facilitation.

chapter 7

HEADS OF STATE GIVE VACCINATIONS IN COLOMBIA

While many activities were undertaken, core operations of the Task Force for Child Survival revolved around quarterly meetings with agency representatives. At these sessions, we reviewed what had been done and received ideas on what should be done next.

The People

In retrospect, much of the effectiveness of the Task Force rested with the representatives designated by its five supporting agencies. Because the agency heads had decided to accept the Task Force, the designated representatives knew that results were expected. They were a small group of accomplished people, although individual members changed with time. There were some large egos, as one would expect with such accomplished people, and yet the mix, over time, was exceptionally harmonious.

Ken Warren, who represented the Rockefeller Foundation, was well known in the global health field. He was outgoing, sometimes loud, opinionated, and yet surprisingly open to others' views. He would often cause a divisive explosion early in the meeting by stating an outrageous opinion not shared by many. This would get everyone upset. He would then back down, and somehow this would lead to an even stronger group consensus at the end. I could never tell whether he did this on purpose, but the trick seemed to be to keep everyone talking until a consensus was reached that avoided taking hardened positions. Ken could be counted on to do some of the difficult work, such as gathering and publishing the proceedings of the large meetings and distributing them in a short time. His heart was absolutely committed to improving global health; he read widely and had many ideas. We came to enjoy and appreciate his bombast.

Steve Joseph represented UNICEF. Unlike the others, his boss, Jim Grant, would also often attend the meetings. This was not because Jim did not trust Steve, but because he was so interested he did not want to miss anything. Steve was a global health professional, spoke French, had served in the Peace Corps, and was a tireless worker. Later, when Steve accepted another position, Terrel Hill represented UNICEF and provided a quiet, thoughtful approach to everything and continued the UNICEF tradition of hard work.

Rafe Henderson, from the WHO, has already been mentioned. He had such a direct interest in the success of this group that he is the only representative who served continuously for a dozen years. Because most of the agencies were in New York or Washington, DC, the meetings were usually on the East Coast; yet, Rafe consistently made time to fly from Geneva, Switzerland. He had the keys to the immunization kingdom, knowing what was happening and what was about to happen. His presence was indispensable, and he had always done his homework. He attended thirty-five of the thirty-six core meetings.

William Mashler from United Nations Development Programme (UNDP) and John North from the World Bank attended the initial meetings, but over time they were replaced by Tim Rothermel from UNDP and Tony Measham from the World Bank. Tim knew how to get things done and had wide experience in the global field. The group had deep respect for his views and experience. Tony was a low-key but intense global health professional with a keen interest in population and family planning. He brought a quiet, knowledgeable presence to the meetings.

Soon Newton Bowles from UNICEF began to attend. Newton

had grown up in China, was a friend of Jim Grant, and had a deep affection for UNICEF. He joined Bill Watson as revered father figures for the group. The make-up of this group provided a key ingredient for a productive coalition; the global health community trusted them. Trust is the glue for productive coalitions. It is also the reason the world listens to them.

Such a great group of people, no direct supervision, a positive global environment for immunization acceleration, high expectations from the participants at the Bellagio meeting—and we didn't know what we were doing!

Key Ingredients of Successful Coalitions

I have already mentioned some of the important constituents of successful coalitions. One is having the mandate come from the heads of the groups involved. This we had.

Second is a clear description of the last mile, one's clear objective. In this case, our goal was to reach children with vaccines by 1990. In time, Jim Grant defined that goal for the group and the world as 80 percent coverage. This was a daunting goal, as measles immunization levels had increased from less than 5 percent to 18 percent in the first eight years of the program. In other words, we were talking about quadrupling that coverage goal, but in only six years, not eight years. This called for true acceleration and not following the projected line.

The third key feature of our coalition was ego suppression. The heads of UNICEF and the WHO had already decreed that there would be no ego expansion in the Task Force. Our job was to facilitate but never compete with the agencies. Whether we could balance the need for executive leadership (making decisions) and congressional leadership (getting everyone on board before making decisions) was yet to be seen.

Another element was optimism. Doubters do not achieve great objectives. Pessimists rarely excel. We would occasionally have some pessimists in the core group, but they never lasted long. They became uncomfortable.

Our first meeting of the small group of representatives of the five agencies was held two months after the Bellagio meeting, hosted at the World Bank. The minutes of the meeting recorded "tempered optimism," with the report I gave on the steps that had been taken to date. We had a long way to go.

Early Decisions

Within the first two meetings, some major agreements were reached on ground rules. First, the group agreed to the Task Force's affiliation with Emory University to provide needed services and with the CDC for technical assistance. This arrangement simplified much of the work to be done.

Second, we clarified the roles of the five sponsoring agencies. UNICEF would be the lead administrative agency for the Task Force, providing the needed support within the UN system. The UNDP resident representative in each country would be involved in any country activities, consistent with the way the UN operates. Third, the WHO would be the lead technical agency, providing the template for scientific guidelines related to child health.

These were logical decisions, but they had to be discussed and agreed to before further steps were possible. The group agreed with the immunization coverage objective, but already the objective was going through a nuanced change, with immunization coverage being seen as the surrogate for the real goal of reductions in morbidity and mortality. If the measurement tools for coverage were bad, and they were, the tools for measuring reductions in morbidity and mortality were abysmal. Therefore, to have a somewhat measurable goal, we talked about "coverage," while in our minds we were substituting "disease incidence."

The group struggled with whether the Task Force should be involved in mobilizing resources—money, donated vaccines, and the like. It was decided that, whenever possible, the Task Force should not be tasked with raising funds. Fortunately, resources soon flowed in, which settled the question.

Although the Task Force was new and untested, surprisingly others wanted to join. The most insistent in this regard was the US Agency for International Development (USAID), which did not want to be left behind when decisions were being made on immunization. Turning this agency down was very hard, especially with its budget of $75 million for child survival, but if it were allowed to join, how could we exclude other bilateral agencies?

It was decided that we would restrict the Task Force core to the five agencies. That required finding ways to communicate activities and encourage feedback from other agencies. We decided on repeat Bellagio meetings, at which other groups could hear reviews and contribute ideas for the future. It was the correct and efficient decision.*

Finally, because administrative matters often lead to unending discussions, Steve Joseph suggested that we always start meetings by discussing substance, strategy, and programs and leave administrative matters to late in the day, when people would be eager to catch flights. That worked.

The Dynamics

First, some comments made by Rafe Henderson in his memoir:

> The Task Force was a remarkable creation not the least because it was illegal. Well, at least in the eyes of our WHO lawyers! I spent many weeks in drafting and re-drafting "Memoranda of Understanding," the normal basis for formalizing cooperation among different UN agencies. None were acceptable. Our lawyers could not countenance including the Rockefeller Foundation, a private entity outside of the UN's purview, in the agreement. (No other agencies seemed to have problems, but I think this simply may have reflected benign neglect.) So we all did without any formal agreement. The actions by our respective organizations were all voluntary in any case, the only real

*Some years later, others made an attempt to institute a similar task force for HIV/AIDS. Dozens of agencies were made part of the core group. It proved impossible to reach decisions with such a large group, and the effort was abandoned.

obligation being to pay a contribution of some $250,000 per biennium to provide for the secretariat . . .

The Task Force functioned admirably as a neutral catalyst among these agencies. It had no authority to coordinate or to implement and did not compete with them for funding. We met (quarterly) . . . for one day, most often in New York City, where three of the co-sponsors were headquartered. We could, and did, talk frankly without needing to be defensive. We often started with a wide-ranging discussion of broad health matters, helped by data that the secretariat had summarized. And that led us to discuss how our individual organizations might help promote actions supporting immunization as well as other aspects of child survival and development. (1)

Part of the secret, therefore, was informality. The fact that the WHO could not figure out a legal way to incorporate us into their activities is a reflection of the tight restrictions on that organization and suggests how useful an "outlaw" group might be. The broad interest in child health was consistent with Mahler's desire to have immunization contribute to primary health care and not just be an isolated and vertical program. These discussions would often lead to requests for more information. The secretariat had the entire CDC to tap to assemble that information for the next meeting.

The dynamics of expressing feelings openly, the tension that might then develop, and finally the resolution that provided a sigh of relief for all, led time after time to increased confidence that we could find solutions. Indeed, the ability to resolve issues amicably led both UNICEF and the WHO to insert items beyond immunization for discussion at the meetings.

Solving Problems

After a general review of child health issues, the discussions often revolved around barriers to immunization. Ultimately, UNICEF and the WHO were able to issue several joint publications, and they became widely used. It would appear from the outside that such collaboration should have been easy. The truth is that over the years many ridiculous obstacles had been erected. For example, training UNICEF staff was forbidden by the WHO; likewise, UNICEF would not accept training from the WHO. The creation of the Task Force changed some of these historical problems. When the WHO developed training materials for immunization and actually conducted training courses for UNICEF, Rafe simply called them briefing sessions rather than training sessions. The foibles of people and the power of turf cannot be overestimated.

Some things had to be ignored. Throughout the years, the WHO program was known as EPI, the Expanded Programme on Immunization, while in UNICEF it became known as UCI, Universal Childhood Immunization. The possessiveness of titles was not worth fighting about.

Grant had developed the term *Universal Childhood Immunization* and therefore it had great power. As Rafe Henderson has written,

> [Grant] had proclaimed that this could be "the leading edge" of the "Child Survival Revolution" launched in 1983 with the first of UNICEF's State of the World's Children reports. Of course, this caused both annoyance within WHO and general confusion for the staffs of our two organizations. We all had to scramble to devise the explanation that UCI represented the immunization goal, while the EPI was the program through which the goal was to be achieved. (Whew!) (1)

One by one, the group found solutions to the usual irritations that cause agencies to ignore, fight, or undermine one another.

Smoke and Mirrors

As productive as these sessions were, smoke and mirrors were also involved. The donor community was lulled into thinking we were actually developing global plans, while in truth, we were still trying to identify the barriers to improved immunization coverage. Resources began to increase for immunization (not for the Task Force but for all of the agencies already involved in immunization programs), and therefore it became necessary to quickly develop global objectives and plans. McNamara's assertion that one hundred million new dollars would change the entire global program had been roundly criticized at the Bellagio meeting as being unrealistic. Two years after that meeting, no one would have settled for $100 million. Italy alone pledged $100 million (ultimately raised to $120 million) for UNICEF to use in immunization programs in Africa. The Western European UNICEF committees mounted an effort to raise an additional $100 million. Some things have to be believed to be seen, and the global immunization community had become believers. Steve Joseph reported that UNICEF was gratified by the support generated. An understatement, to be sure.

Work was initiated with India when that country requested assistance in improving its vaccine production capacity, support with outside vaccine until its production met its needs, and assistance with cold-chain problems. UNICEF and the WHO responded to these requests. In Senegal, UNICEF provided short-term assistance by assigning Mark LaPointe, an experienced CDC field-worker, to assist in developing that country's program.

Colombia's Success: A President Gets Involved

Colombia provided the first real success. The combination of Colombian president Belisario Betancur Cuartas, the Pan American Health Organization (PAHO), and support from UNICEF led to very productive immunization days. PAHO was spurred on by the extraordinarily productive Ciro de Quadros, who had worked in smallpox eradication and now headed the immunization program in the Americas. He pioneered many tactics adopted worldwide.

I observed the third special immunization day, held in Colombia on August 24, 1984 (less than six months after the Bellagio meeting), when 900,000 children were immunized in a single day. The whole country was truly mobilized: the military was involved, together with merchants, schools, parents, and civic organizations. Priests included immunization messages in their sermons on the Sunday preceding each round of immunizations. On the day devoted to mass immunizations, President Betancur gave the first polio immu-

Colombian President Belisario Betancur Cuartas handing President Jimmy Carter a dose of oral polio vaccine to administer to a child in Colombia, 1985. Photo courtesy The Jimmy Carter Presidential Library and Museum

nization at 8 a.m., televised from his home, and with that, the clinics began to immunize.

I was a spectator when President Betancur gave the first immunization. I remarked to him that only one American president, up to that time, had ever given a vaccine. He wanted to know which one, and I told him it was Thomas Jefferson, who administered the smallpox vaccine. I did not know that President Betancur was a Jeffersonian scholar, but he then took me to his library to show me shelves of books on Jefferson. He later invited President Carter to participate in administering vaccines so that there would be two US presidents in that category.

Colombia invited the Task Force to Cartagena for the second Bellagio conference in the fall of 1985. The invitation was accepted. The meeting was to be sponsored by the Task Force and hosted by Colombia. This was the first indication that the Task Force had the power to do things within *days* that would have required *months* of negotiation if each agency had needed to be involved.

Opportunities Everywhere

The value of the Task Force was also demonstrated in its ability to respond to requests quickly. When Ethiopia requested 50,000 doses of measles vaccine and jet injectors to combat a measles outbreak, the Task Force was able to respond within forty-eight hours with the help of the CDC and the WHO. The value of the Task Force was the ability to combine the responses of various agencies, surpassing what the agencies might be able to accomplish individually. Without the usual bureaucratic restraints, rapid response was possible.

The Task Force could do things within *days* that would have required *months* of negotiation if each agency had needed to be involved.

The core group then focused on research needed to improve immunization programs. When I was director at the CDC, I observed repeatedly that the best people were always seeking ways to improve their work. In other words, applied research was a constant, even though research was not the focus of the CDC's mandate. Ken Warren became the representative to investigate basic research needs. We asked several people to canvas the field for thoughts on the biggest applied research needs. We then assembled a top-ten list. We shared it with everyone we could identify, asking for ideas for the next ten applied research needs. This focused some of the discussion we would have at the Cartagena meeting.

Suddenly, opportunities expanded everyplace. The Task Force was asked to testify at a Senate committee hearing interested in global health. This resulted in increased US government funding to USAID for child survival. USAID, in turn, increased the child survival budget allocation for both UNICEF and UNDP. Sudan requested assistance through Joe Giordano, a consultant with the Task Force. Arrangements were made to send Larry Dodd from the CDC under UNICEF auspices. Dodd was a public health advisor with the CDC's immunization program with impressive credentials as a problem-solving field-worker in the United States and in many other countries.

In early 1985, I was able to report that PAHO was planning a hemisphere-wide campaign to eliminate polio. I chaired PAHO's Inter-Agency Coordination Committee meeting with possible donors, and we quickly identified sufficient resources. At the July 1985 Task Force meeting, I reported on the PAHO progress and asked whether it might be the right time to raise the issue of global polio eradication. Only Ciro de Quadros, attending from PAHO, supported the idea; others in the group voiced concerns that it was too early to suggest such an objective.

The executive board of the International Physicians for the Prevention of Nuclear War voted to promote child health programs as part of its effort to alert the world to think positively about survival, rather than focus only on the negative aspects of nuclear weapons. This group invited me to report on child health efforts at its meetings in Germany and the Soviet Union. The group supported the idea of child survival as an important component for a safer world.

The Task Force was evolving. By July 1985, the five sponsoring agencies saw its tasks as follows: (1) to provide a forum for global agencies to discuss immunization and plan cooperatively, (2) to act as a catalyst for country efforts, and (3) to be a service resource for activities that were difficult for other agencies to do on their own or jointly.

An example of the third objective occurred when the CDC wanted to provide a polio expert to Vietnam but could not because the United States did not have diplomatic relationships with Vietnam. The Task Force was able to use money from the WHO to hire an epidemiologist from France and assign him to Vietnam. His supervision came from the CDC. We simply didn't have the same limitations or rules as large agencies.

As Newton Bowles expressed in his 1998 UN report, the Task Force was

not caught in the sterile formalities of much interagency machinery. In effect, it made itself up as it went along. . . . The work-a-day arrangements that facilitated substantive discussion were exemplary. A formal agenda based on concerns of the whole group or of individual members was circulated in advance. Background papers on important topics were also circulated. A summary report of discussions and decisions was prepared after each meeting and sent to all participants. Within this structured setting, meetings were informal. (2)

With an invigorating year and a half of experience, the Task Force sponsored Bellagio II in Cartagena to review the past actions and to seek consensus on future work.

chapter 8

BELLAGIO II IN CARTAGENA, OCTOBER 1985

Interest in immunization had grown, and the second Bellagio conference, held in Cartagena, Colombia, eighteen months after the first meeting, presented a marked contrast (1). The number of participants increased from thirty-four to eighty-seven. Instead of agonizing over how to improve immunization programs and the lack of potential resources, the conference was dominated by confidence, examples of success, resources that exceeded anyone's expectations, and hope that reaching 80 percent of children in the next five years was actually possible.

Colombian President Betancur gave a positive opening speech. The country hosted the meeting in a beautiful setting. Rarely have I attended an international conference exuding such joy. For a moment, the turf-guarding had stopped, and everyone was in harness together.

Rafe Henderson reported that, in the previous eighteen months, DPT3 (the third dose of DPT) coverage had increased from 31 percent to 38 percent and polio3 (the third dose of polio vaccine) from 24 percent to 33 percent. The real surprise was an increase in measles immunization—from 14 percent to 25 percent, a quarter of the children in the developing world.

Presentations on how immunization was fitting into other pri-

Cover of conference report from Bellagio II, Cartagena, Colombia, October 1985. *Protecting the World's Children: "Bellagio II" at Cartagena, Colombia, October 1985,* Conference Report (Atlanta: The Task Force for Child Survival; New York: The Rockefeller Foundation, 1986)

mary health programs focused with particular interest on diarrheal disease and family planning programs. Basic and applied research presentations gave a glimpse of not only what was likely in the near future but also which applied research problems needed highest priority. These presentations provided an opportunity to feed back the information that had come from many field-workers on what they regarded as the highest applied research needs. From the many suggestions, we had selected the top ten. They clustered in three different areas—engineering, biochemistry, and field and operational research.

Engineering. The world needed inexpensive, self-contained, single-injection devices for vaccine administration. The program also needed simplified cold-chain equipment and small and simple jet injectors.

Biochemistry. More potent vaccines requiring only one or two injections were needed, such as for pertussis. Also needed were high-potency, stable virus vaccines that did not require a cold chain. The need for a cold chain for measles vaccine was a constant headache. We also needed simplified diagnostic methods to test for current or past experience with the diseases involved.

Field research. The greatest short-term results were likely in field and operational research. Research goals aimed to reduce the age at which vaccines could be given; to attempt to deliver all vaccines in only two doses; to improve management, training, surveillance, and evaluation methods; and to improve strategies for polio eradication.

For a moment, the turf-guarding had stopped, and everyone was in harness together.

The conference had the good fortune of having Dr. John Evans as the rapporteur. John was an innovator in education. He had pioneered work in Canada on improving the medical school curriculum. Most medical schools presented a crowded academic agenda for the first two years in biochemistry, histology, anatomy, and the usual subjects a student would need before seeing patients in the third and fourth year of school. That approach was competitive and therefore the advantage went to the student who knew more than others in order to do well on tests. Evans changed the approach to have small clusters of students working on problems. His rationale was that they would learn more through cooperation and sharing knowledge because that is how the real world would operate when they graduated. The approach caught on, and when Harvard changed its curriculum to "Coalition Learning," John Evans headed up an evaluation team to consult on their results. He later worked on global health projects for the World Bank and was sought after by global health agencies because of his wisdom.

Evans's summary remarks captured the magic of this meeting. He said the fact that the heads of WHO, UNICEF, UNDP, Rockefeller Foundation, and the World Bank invested three days in the meeting demonstrated the interest of the global community. He commented on the sense of confidence that now was evident as well as the pragmatic approaches being tried in country programs. He succeeded in commenting on almost every speaker, lifting a phrase or message from the talks, as when he quoted Ghanaian public health physician Fred Sai on the "brushstrokes" of each participant because it is "difficult to paint the whole canvas at once."

Evans talked about successes that were generating other successes. He remarked on the conference's common themes—the role of management, political will, and involvement of the populations affected; motivating health workers; and evaluation.

He talked about the Task Force's acting as a catalyst, a facilitator, a problem solver, and a communicator without being directive or achieving a high profile. The Task Force had provided a space for the agencies to talk in a noncompetitive setting and to generate creative solutions. And without bureaucracy, the Task Force could respond to country requests for advice, personnel, or information by assembling the best ingredients from multiple agencies. Evans concluded that the meeting had been an unusually pleasant international experience with an overriding sense of common purpose (1).

The ten-year investment in immunization by the WHO was now paying off in concrete ways.

chapter 9

AFTER CARTAGENA

As immunizations accelerated, so did the work. On the flight back from Cartagena, Jim Grant suggested we needed a newsletter to keep people informed on the many immunization developments. In a gesture that signified why this enterprise was working so well, he suggested that, if UNICEF published such a newsletter, it might cause jealousies. He recommended that UNICEF give the Task Force for Child Survival money and the Task Force would publish the newsletter. This we did. We called it *WIN*, or *World Immunization News*. It soon developed a distribution list of more than 12,000 people and ultimately reached 15,000 immunization workers. The desire for current information on immunization approaches was beyond expectations.

And money continued to be pledged. Canada announced another $25 million for Commonwealth countries. The major concern at the original Bellagio conference about the lack of resources had receded. The chief problems now were the need for good plans, adequate management, and the absorptive capacity of countries (that is, their ability to responsibly use the resources available from the international community). Surveillance systems also needed to be improved to measure vaccine-preventable health problems. And rigorous evaluation was necessary to determine whether the programs' health problems were improving.

The Task Force focused increasingly on specific problems. The need for evaluation led the WHO and UNICEF to work on a joint evaluation manual. It was published and endorsed by all of the agencies.

The increase in HIV in Africa led to concerns about needle safety. At the time, the only reliable approach was sterilization of needles and syringes, and implementing this approach was exceedingly difficult. The Task Force and the WHO accelerated work on auto-destruct syringes that could only be used once. The WHO issued a request for proposals and pursued the most promising. At our core meetings, we would try to disable the various prototypes. Auto-destruct syringes eventually became the standard approach.

Applied research was badly needed, but the WHO did not have the resources to do this. The Rockefeller Foundation and United Nations Development Programme each offered the Task Force $250,000 a year to organize such studies. However, I thought it important to institutionalize such an effort, so I offered the WHO the $500,000 a year. This provided the resources the WHO needed. The WHO instituted a program with an advisory group, which I chaired. Soon we had more than 200 applied research projects under way.

New vaccines were close to being marketed. One of the most promising was a vaccine against hepatitis B. However, new vaccines were more expensive than the standard vaccines and would require a new effort to seek resources. The hepatitis B vaccine was projected to be $1 per dose or $3 for the series—four times the cost of all the vaccines being administered at the time.

The Task Force's workload was increasing because we were being asked to do so many things. But people were willing to pay us to fulfill their requests, so we added short-term and long-term personnel, including Joe Giordano, George Rubin, Hector Traverso, and Seth Berkley. We often had to turn away requests for new projects and never had to conduct fund-raising. The core members urged us not to expand the Task Force into a large agency.

In April 1986, I told the Task Force members at our quarterly meeting that I had been asked to become executive director of the Carter Center. I had accepted, and President Carter agreed to the same terms negotiated with the CDC, namely, that the Carter Center would pay my entire salary, and I could have up to half of my time to work at the Task Force. To simplify the arrangement, and to avoid having two offices, the Task Force rented space at the Carter

Center. It turned out to be a good arrangement, as it permitted us to call on President Carter for assistance, and, at the same time, he became deeply immersed in global health programs. This experience solidified another lesson learned. Every public health decision is ultimately based on a political decision. Public health workers need to be involved in politics, and President Carter showed us how it could be done.

The Task Force helped to sponsor studies of two measles vaccines in Senegal, the Edmonston-Zagrab strain and the high-titer Schwarz strain. John Bennett, a CDC infectious disease specialist as well as an exceptional scientist and an imaginative thinker, came to the Task Force and supervised these studies. The objective was to find a vaccine that could be given before nine months of age to provide immunity before a child's first exposure to wild measles virus.

Public health workers need to be involved in politics; President Carter showed us how that could be done.

As the country's immunization programs strengthened, exploring how this structure could benefit primary health care beyond immunizations became important. The possibility of adding iodine and vitamin A to immunization programs was also explored at various meetings. Programs were encouraged to experiment with ways of providing these vital child health ingredients as part of the immunization activities. In addition, the WHO and UNICEF prepared a joint statement on the use of vitamin A for children with measles.

Dr. Ben Rubin, who developed the bifurcated needle while working for Wyeth, gave a presentation on a simplified jet injector that could run on a nine-volt battery. The Rockefeller Foundation pledged to seek funds for this project. Ideas and projects were coming in daily.

At the September 1987 quarterly Task Force meeting of the five sponsors, it was announced that for the first time coverage for the third doses of either DPT3 or polio3 had exceeded 50 percent. As always, these figures demonstrated improvement but also required us to face how many children were not reached.

Jim Grant was eager to have a third Bellagio meeting in early 1988 to keep agencies informed of the rapid progress of immunization programs and the success of the polio program in the Americas. (It now anticipated interrupting transmission of polio by 1990.) This meeting could also provide a final push before planning a "Summit for Children" in late 1990. He agreed to contact the other agency heads.

In October 1987, the Task Force conducted a dinner at the Carter Center, sponsored by the US Committee for UNICEF, to raise money for child survival. It was such a success that it was repeated annually. Each year attendance increased until we were holding the event in Atlanta's Swiss Hotel for a capacity crowd of 700 people. For speakers, we were able to attract President Carter, Ambassador Andrew Young, actress Liv Ullmann, actor Peter Ustinov, television personality Hugh Downs, and actress Audrey Hepburn, herself a UNICEF Goodwill Ambassador. Being able to attract such people was one additional benefit of being housed at the Carter Center.

By January 1988, Rafe Henderson reported that the WHO now calculated that the Accelerated Immunization Programme (EPI) prevented 1 million deaths a year. He reported that WHO's Expanded Programme on Immunization Global Advisory Group planned to discuss global polio eradication at the next year's meeting. (This discussion would be preempted by a World Health Assembly resolution four months later.)

In January 1988, I reported to the quarterly Task Force meeting that I had agreed with Merck & Co. to chair an expert committee to guide Merck's donation of Mectizan for the treatment of onchocerciasis (river blindness). This turned into a major program that continues to this day (see Chapter 16).

The January quarterly meeting of the Task Force then considered at length the upcoming Bellagio III meeting to be held in Talloires, France.

chapter 10

BELLAGIO III IN TALLOIRES, FRANCE, MARCH 1988

The third Bellagio meeting was held at the Tufts University European Center in Talloires, France, March 10-12, 1988 (1). Because of space limitations, only sixty people could be accommodated. In his memoirs (2), Rafe Henderson describes the tensions of the first night:

It had an inauspicious start. Talloires, on Lake Annecy, France, is within a couple of hours driving distance from Geneva. Bill Foege had stopped in Geneva on his way to Talloires, and I drove him and a couple of others to the meeting. We left in plenty of time for Bill's opening speech before dinner. I was a little disconcerted to find that the battery in my BMW (which to that point had functioned perfectly) was barely charged enough to start. But start it finally did and off we went.

As dusk was gathering, we reached the French frontier only to find traffic stopped. The frontier guards had gone on strike! I did not dare to stop the car because of worries about the battery. But I also had a fuel problem, as I had not filled up prior to departure, although I had plenty of gas for an uninterrupted trip. And what to do about Bill's speech?

Happily, the work stoppage lasted only a little more than an hour and both the battery and the gas held out. Of course, no one carried

The Task Force for
Child Survival

Protecting the
World's Children:
An Agenda for the 1990s

March 10-12, 1988

Tufts University European Center
Talloires, France

Cover of conference report from Bellagio III child survival conference, Talloires, France, March 10-12, 1988. *Protecting the World's Children: An Agenda for the 1990s,* Conference Report (Atlanta: Task Force Child Survival, 1998)

cell phones then so we could not warn anyone of our delay. When we finally did arrive, we found that all the talks had been postponed until after dinner, and the evening went off without a hitch.

At the meeting, Rafe announced that DPT3 and polio3 were now reaching half of all children in the developing world. What's more, 37 percent of children were receiving the measles vaccine, up from

25 percent at the Cartagena meeting just two-and-a-half years before. Solid results were observed from most countries.

I presented data on global trends, much of it assembled by John Bennett. Some of the most interesting statistics showed marked reductions in infant and childhood mortality in the previous twenty-five years. Counterintuitively, the percentage drop in mortality was highest in countries that started with the lowest rates of mortality; we had expected that the countries with the highest mortality would see the most significant drop.

In 1986, some 39,000 children under the age of five years were dying each day, a figure that added up to 14.3 million children a year. Clearly, this was an absolutely discouraging number. And yet if we had been living with the mortality rates of 1960, the figure would have been 70,000 per day or 25.4 million per year. The improvement in rates meant 11.1 million children did not die in 1986 because of improvements in child survival activities.

Surprising Findings on Births

John Bennett had calculated that, while birth *rates* had been decreasing for some years, birth *numbers* were continuing to increase, with about 130 million births a year—because these countries had such high numbers of people of childbearing age. But Bennett projected that numbers of births would peak in 1995 (with more than 140 million births)—and then begin to decrease (3).

This, if true, was a critical finding. The global immunization program had always had its critics, who maintained that we were making the population problem worse and that, therefore, the world would ultimately suffer more. Bennett's data suggested otherwise. Surprised by these results, Bennett called the World Bank to make sure his calculations were correct and were based on the best statistics available. The statistician he talked to was doubtful and asked which data set Bennett was using. "The World Bank data set," Bennett answered. The statistician called later to tell John he was correct and that the World Bank statistician had missed this interpretation. The implications of Bennett's analyses and projections were very important.

The belief that the child survival movement would just increase population problems was not true. Indeed, the converse turned out to be true. The *fastest* population growth rates are seen in the countries with the *highest* infant and childhood mortality rates. The *lowest* growth rates are in the countries with the *lowest* infant and

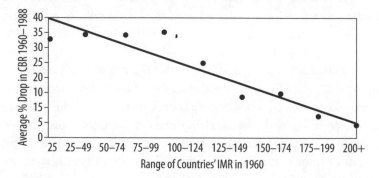

Global changes in crude birth rates (CBR), 1960–1988, by the initial infant-mortality rate (IMR) range. The lower the IMRs, the greater the decline in birth rates. Reducing infant deaths does not lead to higher birth rates of the population. John Bennett, Task Force for Child Survival

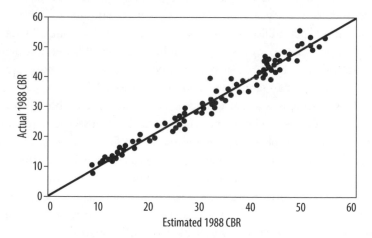

Projected vs. actual crude birth rates, 1988, based on 1980 infant-mortality rates (IMR) and 1970-1980 trends. IMRs can be used to predict future birth rates accurately. John Bennett, Task Force for Child Survival

childhood mortality rates. The best predictor of birth rates is the
recent trend in infant mortality (3). Put bluntly, when a couple's children keep dying, they keep having more; when their children all
live, they do not have large families. High childhood mortality is a
tragedy, but it is also ineffective in controlling population growth.
Even with high infant and child mortality, birth rates continue to be
so high that they fuel population growth.

Presentations covered a range of child survival activities in addition to immunization. A series of countries reported on their programs, and donor agencies reported on their hopes and plans for the
future. D. A. Henderson, as rapporteur, gave a compelling summary
of what had occurred and what it meant for the primary care revolution.

Rotary Has a Dream

Two major developments marked this as an incredibly important
meeting in the history of global health. Together in this secluded
setting, ministers of health from some of the largest countries in
the world were able to discuss the scientific basis for polio eradication. They also heard from Herb Pigman, who had served as general
secretary of Rotary International and the Rotary Foundation from
1979 to 1986. Pigman talked about Rotary's vision to help to eradicate polio. Three years earlier, the Rotary Foundation had pledged
to raise $120 million to eliminate polio from the world. The organi-
zation was able to mobilize Rotarians around the world to donate
money and time to support local polio eradication efforts. Pigman
then went off-script to say to the ministers that they would meet
Rotarians in their countries so excited by the Rotary role that "you
would think they had invented vaccines." He asked the ministers
to be kind to them because they were truly there to help. Pigman's
heartfelt words were galvanizing. Two months later, ministers of

health from throughout the world passed a resolution at the World Health Assembly, asking the WHO to undertake global polio eradication.

There was some background to this Task Force on Child Survival meeting and the World Health Assembly meeting two months later that participants did not know at the time. The WHO was reluctant to get involved in polio eradication this early for a number of valid reasons, including wanting to evaluate the experience in the Americas before expanding the effort and hoping to establish a strong immunization program before accepting another task.

High childhood mortality is a tragedy, but it is also ineffective in controlling population growth.

However, two months before the Talloires meeting, the WHO executive board had nominated Dr. Hiroshi Nakajima as its next director-general. There were serious questions about his abilities, however; and, in fact, he proved to be a major disappointment as a WHO leader. So Jim Grant approached the current director-general, Halfdan Mahler, to see whether the WHO would speed up the timetable and endorse polio eradication before Nakajima took office. Mahler sought Rafe Henderson's advice. Rafe answered that while he would prefer to wait, because Nakajima would be elected at the meeting, Rafe would support the polio eradication goal. So the Talloires ministers had reached scientific agreement to propose eradication but would not know until later why their bold proposal fell on receptive ears at the WHO two months later.

The other major development at Talloires was that Rafe Henderson, with the help of other people from key WHO programs, had drawn up a list of objectives that they hoped could be achieved by the year 2000 in the primary health care area. This was a creative attempt to give specifics to the Alma-Ata dreams, first promulgated in 1978 (see chapter 3).

The Talloires conference attendees were in such an upbeat mood that they readily supported a series of goals. In a two-page Declaration of Talloires (2), they included the plea to countries and health

Millennium Development Goals

According to Wikipedia and UNICEF's Millennium Development Goals (MDG) website, eight international development goals were officially established following the Millennium Summit of the United Nations in 2000, after the United Nations Millennium Declaration was adopted. All 193 UN member states and at least twenty-three international organizations agreed to achieve these goals by 2015. The goals are:

1. Eradicating extreme poverty and hunger
2. Achieving universal primary education
3. Promoting gender equality and empowering women
4. Reducing child-mortality rates
5. Improving maternal health
6. Combating HIV/AIDS, malaria, and other diseases
7. Ensuring environmental sustainability
8. Developing a global partnership for development

Each goal has specific targets and dates for achieving those targets. To accelerate progress, the G8 (the group of eight highly industrialized countries—France, Germany, Italy, the United Kingdom, Japan, the United States, Canada, and Russia) finance ministers agreed in June 2005 to provide enough funds to the World Bank, the International Monetary Fund, and the African Development Bank to cancel an additional $40 billion to $55 billion debt owed by members referred to as the heavily indebted poor countries, or HIPC. This action would allow impoverished countries to rechannel resources saved from the forgiven debt to social programs for improving health and education and for alleviating poverty.

The Sustainable Development Goals (SDGs) followed the MDGs in 2016.

Source: Millennium Development Goals, available from Wikipedia.org, accessed May 29, 2017.

organizations that they attempt to achieve the following by the year 2000. Here are some summary points from the declaration:

1. The global eradication of polio.
2. The virtual elimination of tetanus.
3. A 90 percent reduction in measles cases and a 95 percent reduction in measles deaths as compared to pre-immunization levels.
4. A 70 percent reduction in the 7.4 million annual deaths due to diarrhea in children under the age of five years, when compared to the period before oral rehydration therapy was given.
5. A 25 percent reduction in case-fatality rates associated with acute respiratory infections in children under five years of age.
6. Reduction of infant and under-five child mortality rates by at least half (1980–2000) or to 50 and 70 per 1,000 live births, respectively, whichever would achieve the greater reduction.
7. Reduction of current maternal mortality rates in all countries by at least half.

As Rafe Henderson has pointed out, this is what Grant wanted from the world Summit for Children to be held in two years. This started the dialogue. As Rafe phrased it in his memoirs (1), "This was the first time to my knowledge that such a set of development targets had been put in a document purported to represent a consensus of the international health community. These targets were the beginnings of what would become the health component of the 'Millennium Development Goals' established following the Millennium Summit of the United Nations in 2000."*

*The origin of this process may actually have started a decade earlier, in White Hall at Emory University in 1978. Surgeon General Julius Richmond and Assistant Surgeon General Mike McGinnis had been advocating for 1990 quantitative goals for public health in the United States.

At this meeting, we began hammering them out. The next day the meeting continued at the CDC, and we came up with 220 health objectives for the nation to be met by 1990. These were first published in 1979 as *Healthy People: The Surgeon General's Report on Health Promotion and Disease Prevention*. By 1990, we had reached 50 percent of the goals. Twenty-five percent of them we could not yet even measure. Some would call this a failure. But I see it as a great success because we put them on the agenda, and that started a process that continues to this day.

Notice that Rafe says, "a document purported to represent a consensus of the international health community."

The Declaration of Talloires was an important document for many reasons, but for any agency or ministry of health to officially endorse it would have required a lengthy process.

The core Task Force group decided to follow the advice of Wilbur Cohen, former secretary of Health, Education and Welfare during the Eisenhower administration, who used to say, "Sometimes you have to rise above principle." We decided to publish the declaration as a Task Force document. We had no procedure for clearing such a document. We were clear that this was a Task Force document, but of course the global health world assumed it was the statement of the participating agencies and ministries. It did the job and was used as a guide.

In May, two months later, the World Health Assembly met in Geneva, and the resolution calling on the world to eradicate polio was passed.

chapter 11

THE HARVEST OF TALLOIRES

We would have two years before the next meeting, Bellagio IV, in Bangkok, Thailand. It was to be a gathering of health leaders in 1990 in preparation for the Summit for Children, which was to be held later that same year in New York.

Major efforts were focused on this summit to be held at the UN headquarters in September. By then, we were determined to come as close to the 80 percent goal of immunization coverage as possible. Meanwhile research continued.

Breakthroughs in Neonatal Tetanus

John Bennett conducted a study in Pakistan on neonatal tetanus. He found that a major risk factor for this bacterial disease was the application of ghee (clarified butter) to the umbilical cord, a common practice. Later it was learned that ghee is very close to the medium used in the laboratory to grow tetanus, so it became clearer why applying ghee to an umbilical cord was a dangerous tradition. This risk factor had not previously been reported and provided an opportunity to implement an intervention project to use substitutes for ghee. Global 2000, a Carter Center program, provided recommendations to President Carter on development projects that could be accomplished before the new millennium.

Neonatal tetanus was a prominent cause of newborn deaths. So it was an absolute shock to find, at least in Pakistan, that global health experts had not suspected ghee as the culprit for such deaths.

The finding led Dr. Bennett to research whether a similar problem existed in Bangladesh. To his surprise, he found cases of neonatal tetanus in children of mothers who had received tetanus toxoid during pregnancy. This was most unexpected. It has been known for years that successful vaccination in pregnancy provides passive antibodies across the placenta, protecting newborns from tetanus.

The investigation became increasingly bizarre. Soon it revealed vaccinated mothers who did not have antibodies. It was then found that the tetanus toxoid being used contained no antigen. The vaccine, which had been made in-country, was inert.

This was a public health emergency. The Task Force for Child Survival recommended the collection of all tetanus toxoid vaccine in Bangladesh and the replacement of vaccine with emergency vaccine supplies provided by the WHO. To our surprise and consternation, the country and the WHO representative decided to continue using the impotent vaccine until it was finished and to fill the pipeline behind that vaccine with good vaccine supplied by the WHO. In other words, a deliberate decision was made to save face by not saving lives. It was one of the most egregious mistakes I have witnessed in global health.

Other Eradicable Diseases?

With smallpox eradicated and two programs under way to eradicate polio and Guinea worm, the question arose concerning future eradication possibilities. The Dana Foundation provided funds to the Carter Center for an ad hoc Task Force on Disease Eradication to determine what might be possible. I asked Dr. Don Hopkins to chair the group, which attempted to review all infectious diseases. Dr. Hopkins was the perfect chair: he had a medical degree, a degree in public health, board certification in pediatrics, and fieldwork in

Africa and India. It was his initiative to eradicate Guinea worm, a debilitating parasitic disease caused by infection with the largest parasite known to plague people, the up-to-3-foot-long Guinea worm. (It is also the single biggest reason for school absenteeism in Nigeria. One of the most startling cases I ever saw was in a six-month-old, unusual because the incubation period is twelve months. Clearly, the parasite crossed the placenta.) That effort, in turn, was uncovering nonvaccine interventions to eliminate the disease.

Instead of asking the usual question about whether a disease could be eradicated, the question was changed to, "What would be required to eradicate the disease?" This totally changed the perspective and provided a research agenda for diseases potentially eradicable in the future. For example, it was felt that measles eradication was thwarted by the inability to give vaccine before about nine months of age. Early transmission of measles in Africa led to the conclusion that a vaccine usable even three months earlier than that might change the equation. Therefore, a research agenda to develop such a vaccine might make measles eradication potentially achievable.

The CDC, and then the WHO, published the work of this committee. The committee has continued to update the list of potential diseases for eradication as new scientific findings develop.

Hepatitis, Family Planning, and Mectizan

A report by Jim Maynard, a physician formerly with the CDC and a world-class authority on hepatitis, was especially exciting. He told the group that the hepatitis B vaccine, recently down to $1 a dose, or $3 for the series required for protection, could turn out to be half that price. Inclusion of this vaccine in the global program was becoming more likely.

The United Nations Population Fund asked to join the Task Force. It was decided to invite representatives from this program to attend some meetings before deciding on this request. The program was later added to the core group.

At the September 1989 Task Force meeting, Dr. Nakajima attended and talked about his avid interest in child survival programs. The interest may have been there, but he lacked the ability to cooperate with other agencies. The excellent support of Dr. Halfdan Mahler during the previous five years was proving difficult to sustain.

Instead of asking whether a disease could be eradicated—the question was changed to, "What would be required to eradicate the disease?" This totally changed the perspective.

At the same meeting, we could announce that the Task Force had delivered its first shipment of Mectizan. The program to prevent river blindness was under way. By April 1990, we announced shipments of Mectizan to fourteen countries. By October, shipments were going to twenty-three countries.

On April 6, 1989, the Task Force was asked to testify at a hearing on child survival before the Select Committee on Hunger in the US House of Representatives. Jim Grant testified, followed by Audrey Hepburn. Her testimony was heard by a full committee. Following her testimony, the entire committee left, and I testified to the staffers left behind! Good public health is based on good political decisions, and often those decisions involve people of high popularity. Another example of this phenomenon was when Ted Turner asked the Task Force for materials to advertise child survival to use on CNN. UNICEF provided him materials from the Facts for Life Project. (This paperback publication by UNICEF, the WHO and UNESCO, among others, provided practical, low-cost, family-based ways to protect children's lives and health. Properly informing parents and families of the facts in this seventy-five page manual could save millions and drastically reduce malnutrition. It was available in many languages.)

At the next quarterly Task Force meeting on January 4, 1990, we learned that Rafe Henderson had been promoted to assistant director-general of the WHO. He continued to attend Task Force meetings, as immunization was still under his direction. Dr. Robert Kim-Farley took Rafe's place on the EPI program.

chapter 12

BANGKOK'S MESSAGES FOR WORLD LEADERS

On March 1, 1990, more than one hundred health leaders, including twenty ministers of health from developing countries, met in Bangkok. They had three objectives: (1) to identify remaining barriers to achieving the 80 percent immunization goal by the end of the year, (2) to reach consensus on other health goals to be achieved by 2000, and (3) to formulate key messages for the global leaders who would be meeting in September for the first-ever worldwide summit on a social issue, the Summit for Children (1).

The messages were very positive. Immunization coverage had already surpassed 80 percent in thirty-eight countries. The world as a whole had now reached 70 percent to 75 percent of children with at least one vaccine, an increase from less than 20 percent at Bellagio I. More than 2 million children were escaping death each year because of vaccines alone.

Participants felt pressure to capitalize on the next six months before the summit with bold efforts to make this "near miracle a *real* miracle," as one attendee phrased it. Workshop and plenary sessions attempted to define the messages that health leaders would like to hear from heads of state at the summit (2). Ministers of health were urged to help prepare the statements for the heads of state that would be accurate and yet seek to go beyond the standard, conservative goals often expressed.

The conference summary indicated the overriding theme of the Bangkok conference: readiness. The extraordinary advances in the previous six years and the cooperative network that had been developed both suggested that this was a favorable time to try to actually change the priorities of the world.

> The fact that priests in Colombia ask a child's parents at baptism if the child is immunized . . . that Rotary International pledged to raise $120 million to fight polio but raised $240 million instead . . . that the Heads of State of Ghana, Colombia, and Tunisia, among others, actively participated in their country's immunization days . . . surely these are more than signs that the world is no longer willing to tolerate 40,000 children's deaths a day. In the terminology of statisticians and clinicians, these are valid indicators of a bedrock commitment to children. (1)

Children Should Thrive, Not Just Survive

The group had moved far beyond child survival to help define not only survival but also a rational future for children. It had literally turned the spotlight on children. As William H. Draper III, administrator of United Nations Development Programme put it, "Let's turn to the essential task of development. Let's invest in our future. Let's invest in our children, in their survival and in their development." Dr. U. Ko Ko, regional director of the WHO's Regional Office for Southeast Asia, poignantly recalled being present in 1984 when the minister of health of a country in the Indian subcontinent said to his prime minister, "Your children are surviving but not thriving."

- -
The Bangkok participants were emboldened. They no longer wanted a "near miracle but a *real* miracle": to change the priorities of the world.
- -

PROCEEDINGS

PROTECTING
THE
WORLD'S CHILDREN:

A Call for Action

the Fourth International Child Survival Conference
Bangkok, Thailand, March 1-3, 1990

The Task Force for Child Survival

Sponsoring Agencies
of The Task Force
For Child Survival

WHO   UNICEF   World   UNDP   RF
                  Bank

Cover of conference proceedings from Bellagio IV child survival conference, Bangkok, Thailand, March 1-3, 1990. *Protecting the World's Children: A Call for Action,* Proceedings (Atlanta: Task Force for Child Survival, 1990)

This sentiment was not unique among world leaders. As Stephen Umemoto, deputy regional director for UNICEF's East Asia and Pakistan Office, said to the packed auditorium, "Our Heads of Government [and] State tend to view child concerns and resources for children as charity, something we do out of the goodness of our hearts—but not [as something which is] at the core of development and progress for the nation. It is at the core" (1).

Countries Setting New Priorities

So the discussions went beyond immunization and other child health topics. The important findings of John Bennett—that reducing infant deaths does not lead to higher birth rates of the population, but quite the contrary—were discussed (1, 3). (See figures on page 62 in chapter 10.) A considerable time was devoted to women's health because it can't be separated from child health. (In developing nations, the death of a mother in childbirth is usually a death sentence for the child, also.) Two years or more between the births of children is beneficial to both the health of the mother and the health of the child. And female literacy is actually a public health issue. Not only does it benefit the health and welfare of women but also every percentage increase in literacy rates is accompanied by a reduction in infant mortality rates.

A report was given at the conference on the impact of cease-fire days in conflict areas and the ability to improve immunization rates

---

We Can Afford It

UNICEF director Jim Grant said that low-cost solutions to child health problems could prevent 100 million child deaths in the next decade for a cost of $2.5 billion a year. That amount, in 1990, was

- as much as US companies spent each year to advertise cigarettes.
- as much as the Soviet Union spent on vodka each month.
- 2 percent of the poor world's own arms spending.
- the approximate cost of five Stealth bombers.
- 10 percent of the European Economic Community's annual subsidy to its farmers.
- as much as the developing world was paying every week to service its debt.
- as much as the world as a whole spent on the military *every day.*

Source: UNICEF, *The State of the World's Children* (New York: UNICEF, 1989).

---

during those cease-fires. On three separate Sundays during 1985, El Salvador's civil war was stopped to allow a nationwide immunization campaign to protect more than 60 percent of the nation's children.

Jim Grant, executive director of UNICEF, shared some information from the latest *State of the World's Children* report (4). An investment in the proposals of the previous conference in Talloires could be achieved for about $2.5 billion a year and would save 10 million lives a year. (For what that amount bought in 1990, see the box on page 76, "We Can Afford It.") "It is impossible to accept for one moment the notion that the world cannot afford to prevent the deaths and the malnutrition of so many millions of its young children," Grant said (1).

"Affirmation of Bangkok"

The key points of agreement from the discussions were incorporated into the "Affirmation of Bangkok" (5). It appeared in the colorful, twenty-four-page conference report, packed with haunting images of children from throughout the world. (One depicted a father, walking with his son, carrying the coffin of another child on his shoulder.) The medium was the message: we need to see the faces behind the statistics.

The conference report was published and widely disseminated immediately after the conference, so that the key messages could get to heads of state quickly before the Summit for Children in the fall. Had the document gone through clearance procedures within the sponsoring agencies, meeting this time sensitivity would have been nearly impossible. So the Task Force for Child Survival was asked to publish it as a statement from the Task Force, rather than from the agencies. But once again, many felt the "Affirmation of Bangkok" had come from the agencies because those agencies sponsored the Task Force.

The affirmations contained within the "Affirmation of Bangkok" included, among others:

1. Recognition of the remarkable progress of the last decade
2. Urging for accelerated efforts so that both immunization and oral rehydration therapy (for diarrhea) could reach 80 percent of children

3. Urging that similar attention be given to other health and development priorities
4. A call for more collaboration such as that experienced with immunization
5. A call for national leaders to support:
   a. Access to education for 80 percent of primary school-age children
   b. Special attention to the health and nutrition of the female child and pregnant and lactating women
   c. The distribution of *Facts for Life* (6)
   d. Attention to the social and health needs of women
   e. A recognition of the centrality of health for development
6. Attention to previous targets:
   a. To reduce maternal mortality by 50 percent from 1990 levels
   b. To reduce infant mortality by one-third from 1990 levels
   c. To reduce under-five-year mortality by one-third from 1990 levels
7. New targets, including:
   a. Reduction of the rate of low birth weight (2.5 kg) to less than 10 percent
   b. Empowerment of women to breastfeed for the first four to six months
   c. Virtual elimination of iodine-deficiency disorders
   d. Virtual elimination of vitamin A deficiency
   e. Reduction of iron deficiency anemia in women by one-third of 1990 levels
8. Emphasis on the Talloires targets for measles, tetanus, and diarrheal diseases
9. Environmental targets, including:
   a. Universal access to safe water
   b. Universal access to sanitary means of excreta disposal
   c. Elimination of Guinea worm disease
10. And a pledge to work together in the support of these goals.

There were, nevertheless, harbingers of the end of this harmonious global working relationship. Dr. Nakajima, director-general of the WHO, attended the meeting and said nice things about collaboration. However, the truth, according to others from the WHO, was

Selamawit's Wish

If there was a poster child for the emboldened child survival movement, it was Selamawit. Her story spread after Bangkok.

When she was four years old, someone found Selamawit on the
streets of Addis Ababa, capital city of Ethiopia, then the world's
poorest country.

They asked her what she wanted to be when she grew up.

"I want to be alive," she said.

Her wish made her famous. Her face and haunting words appeared
on millions of posters throughout the world. The poster was even hung
on tents in refugee camps. She became the symbol of a movement.

And she got her wish. In fact, in 1988, at the age of nine, Selamawit addressed the heads of state at the Twenty-Fifth Anniversary
Summit of the Organization of African Unity. Jim Grant introduced
her, noting that she was "fully immunized, of course"—as well as
second in her third-grade class of 100. At the time of the Bangkok
conference, Selamawit was twelve.

Photograph of original Selamawit poster, at the Carter Center's Kirbo Building. Poster from UNICEF; photo of poster by Poul Olson

Source: "Selamawit's Wish," *Protecting the World's Children*, Conference Report
(Atlanta: Task Force for Child Survival, 1990), 11.

that he was offended. He thought the WHO should be in charge of all health matters and resented the involvement of other groups.

Female illiteracy is actually a public health issue. Every percentage increase in literacy rates is accompanied by a reduction in infant mortality rates.

At the meeting Rafe Henderson raised the possibility of a vaccine purchase fund, which would make it easier to buy vaccines in bulk and would be a more dependable way for vaccine manufacturers to anticipate quantities of vaccine required. This is now standard operating procedure. But at Bangkok, Dr. Nakajima took strong exception to the idea and was furious with Rafe for suggesting it without consulting him. The tensions between agencies and people were beginning to reemerge. As I emphasized earlier, trust is the glue of successful coalitions. When new people were appointed to key posts, they did not always have that trust that experience engenders.

One week later, Thailand hosted a global education conference, in some ways the corollary of the International Conference on Primary Health Care at Alma-Ata in 1978. UNICEF was heavily involved. Global approaches to basic problems of inequity were beginning to receive attention from world leaders.

The next six months were focused on preparing for the Summit for Children. In addition to discussions on the summit, the August 16, 1990, meeting of the Task Force core group included three other items of interest:

- Hugh Downs had spoken at the Carter Center fund-raiser for UNICEF; $40,000 was collected for UNICEF's child survival efforts.
- The Mectizan Donation Program had now distributed 1.5 million tablets. Postdistribution surveillance in villages to detect adverse effects was part of the program. Initially, surveillance was for 72 hours, later changed to 48 hours and then 24 hours. Only two types of side effects of consequence had been detected—transient low blood pressure in some recipients and an allergic reaction to the microfilaria destroyed in others. Both were easily treated.

- The CDC reported on studies under way comparing IPV (inactivated polio vaccine) and OPV (oral polio vaccine) vaccines in Africa. This research suggested that polio eradication in Africa might be enhanced by the use of both vaccines. (This would later be an important but contentious issue.)

chapter 13

THE SUMMIT FOR CHILDREN

Never before had there been so many world leaders in a single gathering, according to UNICEF. On September 29-30, 1990, seventy-one heads of state and government—as well as eighty-eight other senior officials, mostly at the ministerial level—met, at the United Nations headquarters in New York City. They were there to discuss the future of child health.

Specifically, they were there to address the two facts that UNICEF director Jim Grant called "the quiet catastrophe." Fact one: that 40,000 child deaths were occurring each day from ordinary malnutrition and disease; that 150 million children lived with ill health and poor growth; and that 100 million six- to eleven-year-olds were not attending school. Fact two: that large-scale trials and studies in many nations in recent years had vastly increased both the world's understanding of the problems and its capacity to solve them.

So, the question at the center of the World Summit was "whether morality would keep step with capacity, whether what *could* now be done *would* now be done" (1). And the eyes of the world were on them. The children's cause was acknowledged by headlines in virtually every country (1).

The pageantry that would ordinarily accompany a gathering of this magnitude was evident. But in addition, a child in national dress escorted each head of state to his or her seat.

Jim Grant addressed the country leaders by announcing that 80 percent of children in the world had now been given at least one vaccine. It was, he said, "the largest peacetime accomplishment that the world had ever seen." It was inspiring, as a spectator, to watch that audience react to the sheer audacity of what had been accomplished.

I have attended world health assemblies and listened to the drone of speeches given by 190 ministers of health. It is a chore to remain focused. At the Summit for Children, heads of state were given just five minutes each to summarize what they had done for children and what they intended to do in the future. Many of their talks had been developed by the ministers of health with whom we at the Task Force for Child Survival had been working. So it was easier to be focused at the summit, both because the talks were short and because we were listening for the words the ministers used. It was almost beyond belief to observe such self-discipline in a room of such egos—they were presidents and monarchs, after all. Seventy of the seventy-one actually stayed within their five minutes. The outlier, Margaret Thatcher, simply said she wasn't going to be held to that rule.

As the day progressed, one could sense the role that positive peer pressure was exerting. No head of state wanted to commit to less than the previous speakers had. When the day ended, the world had a new global commitment to child health. A promise to children.

A press conference was held on the child survival revolution. Dr. Nakajima represented the WHO. UNICEF asked me to represent the Task Force. (Before the press conference, an official from the WHO took me aside and asked me to not excel, so Dr. Nakajima would not look inept. The reason I mention this is that it is always surprising that, with the entire world to choose from, we often get leaders not worthy of representing us and indeed, often harmful to the health of the people selecting them. It is the old question of why governments, organizations, and individuals make decisions that are not in their best interests.)

The leaders present at the summit adopted the "World Declaration on the Survival, Protection and Development of Children," as well as a "Plan of Action" for implementing it in the 1990s (2) (see appendix B). In the document, the world leaders made "an urgent universal appeal—to give every child a better future." The document contrasted the innocence and vulnerability of children with the reality:

> They suffer immensely as casualties of war and violence; as victims of racial discrimination, apartheid, aggression, foreign occupation and annexation; as refugees and displaced children, forced to abandon their homes and their roots; as disabled; or as victims of neglect, cruelty and exploitation.

It listed the shocking statistics on death and disease, including from AIDS.

"These are challenges that we, as political leaders, must meet," the document states. "We do this not only for the present generation, but for all generations to come. There can be no task nobler than giving every child a better future."

This commitment ushered in a decade of high-level commitment to issues concerning children. It also was the catalyst for a series of UN conferences on topics directly related to the health and well-being of children, such as population, the environment, and women's rights.*

*One of these efforts, heralded in the declaration was the Convention on the Rights of the Child, which the United States has still not signed. The only other country that has not is Somalia.

UNICEF director Jim Grant never missed an opportunity to recite this poem.

The Child Cannot Wait
We are guilty of many errors and many
Faults, but our worst crime is abandoning the
Children, neglecting the fountain of life.
Many things we need can wait.
The child cannot.
Right now is the time his bones are being formed,
His blood is being made,
And his senses are being developed.
To him, we cannot answer "Tomorrow."
His name is today.

GABRIELA MISTRAL, Nobel Prize-winning poet from Chile

chapter 14

AFTER THE SUMMIT FOR CHILDREN

With a little trust and a commitment to work together, the global community had shown it could quickly improve the immunization status of the children of the world. Maintenance was a different thing. Persons responsible for program activities changed, and new turf battles began. The 1988 election of Dr. Nakajima as director-general presaged the end of the WHO cooperation on this program. Then, in 1995, the children of the world lost a champion when Jim Grant died. His replacement as UNICEF executive director, Carol Bellamy, told a staff member that "immunization is a Jim Grant thing." Over a number of years, she reduced the UNICEF immunization budget from $183 million per year to $53 million per year. When *Humanosphere* journalist and founder Tom Paulson asked her during a taped interview why UNICEF had allowed the immunization program to suffer in the 1990s, she angrily swore at him, perhaps forgetting that he was taping the conversation, and replied that countries had not provided resources.

Anyone would have had difficulty following Jim Grant, with his vision and ability to raise resources. It is also true that it was not a great time for contributions. However, UNICEF's annual reports show that, while the budget of 1995 was $957 million and only increased to $966 million by 1998, the budget for the most powerful tool to save children, immunization, was reduced.

The Task Force for Child Survival continued on with other activities, but it began to withdraw from immunization in the belief that, unless the two key agency heads were interested, it would be a very difficult endeavor. So the Task Force moved in other directions.

A Conference on Micronutrients to End Hidden Hunger

The Task Force had two additional global meetings. The first, Ending Hidden Hunger, was held in Montreal a year after the Summit for Children. Its goal was to promote improvements in programs for micronutrients, such as iodine, iron, vitamin A, and folic acid.

The role of iodine was well known. This inexpensive element clearly needed to be available during a short but crucial part of fetal life. The lack of tiny amounts of iodine during fetal development was causing a major reduction of IQ points in the world.

Another key micronutrient is vitamin A. Johns Hopkins researcher Dr. Al Sommer revealed the power of this micronutrient. Sommer is an ophthalmologist who received epidemiologic training as an Epidemic Intelligence Service officer at the CDC and later became dean of the Johns Hopkins University Bloomberg School of Public Health. His work on blindness and infant mortality demonstrated that vitamin A not only prevented blindness but also reduced mortality rates in children with measles. In addition, adequate vitamin A could reduce infant mortality in some countries by a third.

Other key micronutrients are iron and folic acid. Insufficient iron leads to anemia and compromised strength and vitality for many, especially women in developing areas throughout Africa, Asia, and South America. And the lack of adequate folic acid was now recognized as important in the development of spina bifida, a congenital defect of the spine in which part of the spinal cord and its meninges are exposed through a gap in the backbone. Lack of adequate folic acid can also cause heart disease.

Abundant information now existed on the adverse effects of deficiencies of these micronutrients; moreover, we had experience in how to deliver them. But the micronutrient field was quite fragmented. Some agencies and individual workers were interested in a single nutrient rather than systems to correct multiple deficiencies. Some had a primary interest in supplementation, for instance, administering vitamin A to children receiving vaccines. Others wished to concentrate on fortification by incorporating the micronutrient into food or drink, such as fluoride in water or iodine in salt. Others wanted to alter seeds. For example, quality protein maize seeds contain nearly double the amounts of the essential amino acids lysine and tryptophan, critically important in children weaned on maize.

The micronutrient movement eventually led to a program a decade later, the Global Alliance for Improvements in Nutrition (GAIN). This is a Swiss foundation headquartered in Geneva, started initially by funding from the Bill & Melinda Gates Foundation. This foundation would be a crucial factor in maintaining some of the programs supported by the Task Force.

Integrating Child Health Services: Field Visits in India

The other global meeting sponsored by the Task Force was held in New Delhi in February 1994. It examined the integration of child health services. It was titled "Achieving Health: New Perspectives on Integrated Services and Their Contributions to Mid-Decade Goals" (1).

A number of innovations marked this meeting. First, many of the 130 attendees made field visits for several days before the meeting. These visits included state and district health workers' demonstrations of child health programs in practice. Participants could now see what the programs looked like in actuality before discussing the theory in Delhi.

- -
The fatalism that infects both villagers and heads of state was beginning to be shed.
- -

Second, it was the first meeting at which the World Bank's landmark report on health and development, the *World Development*

Proceedings

Achieving Health:
New Perspectives on Integrated Services
and Their Contributions to Mid-Decade Goals

February 2 - 4, 1994
New Delhi

THE TASK FORCE FOR CHILD SURVIVAL
AND DEVELOPMENT

Cover of report of child survival conference, New Delhi, India, February 2-4, 1994.
Achieving Health: New Perspectives on Integrated Services and Their Contributions to Mid-Decade Goals, Proceedings (Atlanta: Task Force for Child Survival, 1994)

Report 1993: Investing in Health (2), was available. This publication provided a new metric, Disability Adjusted Life Years, or DALYs, to provide a perspective on both morbidity and mortality. The term includes the concept of years lost prematurely if a person dies; however, it also includes equivalent years of healthy life lost due to morbidity, such as dementia, blindness, and amputations. DALYs therefore permit a way to include both mortality and morbidity in a single number and a new way of calculating the benefits of intervention programs. Some diseases, such as arthritis, cause significant suffering but are rarely listed as the cause of death. This metric allows some comparison of conditions with low mortality, such as arthritis or Guinea worm, with diseases of high mortality, such as meningitis, automobile crashes, or heart disease.

Third, as the meeting's name suggests, it looked at all of the various approaches to child health to ask how best to integrate them. Interdependence was the key concept. The fatalism that infects both villagers and heads of UN agencies was beginning to be shed.

Intellectuals solve problems. Geniuses prevent them. —Einstein

---

Key lessons from the meeting included:

1. The importance of community participation. A Canadian International Development Agency evaluation stated, "Of all the lessons that have been learned about development, none is so unequivocally clear as this: Projects defined and carried out without the active participation of the people they are intended to benefit rarely produce the expected result" (1).
2. Political will is critical.
3. Social norms change. Make the absence of a problem the social norm. For example, we often accept problems, such as measles, as a social norm. With a good vaccine, however, measles no longer needs to be the social norm. Yet many find it hard to take the necessary steps to solve even a serious problem. That's why the real solution is in prevention. As Einstein said, "Intellectuals solve problems. Geniuses prevent them."
4. Every effort must be made to raise the status of women to that of men.
5. Equity is measured in deeds, not words.
6. Synergism works.
7. Quantification is of utmost importance. We must document both the burden of disease but also the change in the burden as the result of programs.
8. In the final analysis, health solutions are delivered in a village, not in Geneva or New York.
9. Ethics must be part of everything we do.

Jim Grant closed the meeting and quoted David Ben-Gurion, the father of Israel and first prime minister of that country, as saying, "In order to be a realist, you have to believe in miracles." The past few years have seen one miracle after another, Grant said. "We are really talking about changing the world" (1).

Last Legacies of the Task Force

So what, finally, was the legacy from the Bellagio meeting of March 1984? Its original objective to improve immunization coverage of children throughout the world was miraculously successful, as Grant said. This was accomplished by having a true partnership of the UN agencies for a decade.

But the legacy is even larger. The Task Force eventually produced a number of movements as well as three programs of multi-billion-dollar importance to global health. These could be labeled unintended consequences. We will explore them in chapter 15.

chapter 15

THE GLOBAL ALLIANCE FOR VACCINES AND IMMUNIZATION

By 1990, thanks to the Task Force for Child Survival coalition, Jim Grant was able to declare the first victory of 80 percent access to vaccinations for the world's children. Many expected this percentage would only continue to rise.

Sadly, eliminating human foibles is difficult, and in the 1990s, this progress ground to a halt. Suddenly, developing countries were struggling to maintain vaccination campaigns, and pharmaceutical companies had no incentive to invest in supplying vaccines to the poorest parts of the world. The immunization cooperation in the 1980s had expanded quickly to become one of the most innovative initiatives in global health and development aid. However, without the support of agency leaders, the progress could not be maintained.

Children born in industrialized countries were receiving an average of eleven to twelve vaccines; children in poor countries received half that number. Nearly 30 million children in developing countries were not fully immunized, and newer, more expensive vaccines, such as hepatitis B vaccine, seemed out of reach for poor countries.

With serious questions being raised about the future of global vaccination efforts, the head of the World Bank, James Wolfensohn, convened a summit of the WHO, UNICEF, academics, health ministers, international agencies, and the pharmaceutical industry in

March 1998. Their agenda? How to get vaccines to children who needed them most.

Six months later Bill and Melinda Gates added to the momentum by hosting a dinner at their home for leading scientists to discuss what could be done to overcome the barriers that prevent millions of children from receiving basic vaccines. Bill and Melinda challenged their guests to come back with proposals for "breakthrough solutions."

In March 1999, the Rockefeller Foundation sponsored a second summit at Bellagio in northern Italy. Some participants still recalled the power of the Task Force, a coalition outside of the usual UN structure. This meeting provided the answer to the Gates challenge. Rather than setting up a new international organization, the existing major players in global immunization—the key UN agencies, leaders of the vaccine industry, representatives of bilateral aid agencies, and major foundations—agreed to work together through a new partnership: the Global Alliance for Vaccines and Immunization (GAVI). Like the Task Force before it, GAVI would be a facilitator for cooperation among groups to pursue their goal of global immunization. GAVI's dream of delivering vaccines to millions of the world's poorest children moved a step closer to reality in November 1999, when the Gates Foundation pledged $750 million over five years to GAVI.

We can't overstate the tendency of people to revert to the need for ego enhancement. One would think that achieving the position of head of a major agency would imply self-confidence, evident in an ability to cooperate with others. But it doesn't. And so the ego needs of the heads of UNICEF and the WHO once again caused children to suffer. The difference this time was that an example existed of what had been possible when both agency heads had suppressed their egos for the sake of children. Some could not forget that time, and in all agencies, including the World Bank, people who had worked with the Task Force longed to see similar cooperation in the future.

Two months after the Gates Foundation's pledge, in January 2000, GAVI was formally launched at the World Economic Forum in Davos, Switzerland. By this time, I was working as an advisor to the Gates Foundation, and I was overjoyed that long-term solutions to vaccine production, distribution, and program assessment were feasible.

By 2003, the commitments to GAVI had topped $1 billion. However, that was actually less growth than expected, given the $750 million given by the Gates Foundation. Privately, I worried that Bill and Melinda Gates would tire of the effort when others were slow to commit. But in the fourth year of GAVI, when the Gates Foundation renewed its commitment for another five years, pledges from elsewhere took off. It was as if the world had just been waiting to see whether the Gates Foundation's commitment was going to be sustained. With the announcement of a renewal of Gates funding, Norway and the United Kingdom immediately announced their own contributions. Since then, GAVI has continued to grow.

By October 2004, GAVI announced that 45 million children had received vaccines because of the organization. An estimated 500,000 lives had been saved.

Within another two years, GAVI was developing approaches far beyond anything that had been contemplated during the Task Force days. GAVI was providing help to strengthen delivery systems both to improve immunization services but also to help improve primary health care in general. It was even providing expensive vaccines to poor countries.

It helped launch the relatively expensive rotavirus vaccine, for example. Rotavirus is a frequent cause of diarrhea in children. It afflicts children throughout the world, but it is lethal in developing countries, where it causes hundreds of thousands of childhood deaths because diarrhea leads to dehydration. The introduction of rotavirus vaccines was a huge boost to child survival programs.

GAVI also ventured into financial solutions, selling bonds to provide immediate resources against future pledges from countries. Partnerships between the public and private sector and the acceleration of vaccine production resulted. GAVI was demonstrating, as the Task Force had fifteen years earlier, that global agencies such as the WHO and UNICEF are important—indeed, they may have no substitute—but they are not sufficient. GAVI was becoming a long-term solution to the temporary solution developed by the Task Force.

GAVI exceeded all expectations. It provides even expensive vaccines to poor countries, sells bonds to provide immediate resources, and has developed a vaccine against a form of meningitis.

On March 8, 2011, GAVI announced that Dr. Seth Berkley had been named as its new CEO. A circle had been completed, as Dr. Berkley had originally been employed by the Task Force, funded by the Rockefeller Foundation, and assigned to Uganda to work on child health programs. As previously noted, he became an important link in alerting the president of Uganda to the AIDS crisis, which led the president to publicize the problem. Dr. Berkley brought country experience, Rockefeller experience, training at the CDC, as well as solid scientific experience from his years as head of the International AIDS Vaccine Initiative.

GAVI continues to exceed all expectations. With the collaboration of public and private agencies, including the Gates Foundation, it has succeeded in developing a vaccine against a type of meningitis (group A meningococcal) that had been a plague of West Africa for years. Swooping in silently every year or two, this disease would suddenly kill tens of thousands of West Africans and instill a fear that used to be rivaled only by smallpox. The vaccine, MenAfriVac, costs only about fifty cents a dose and is one more link in the vaccine chain changing global health.

Pledges to GAVI are now in the billions of dollars per year. Would this organization have developed if there had never been a Task Force? One hopes the need would have been identified in any case, leading to the creation of the organization. However, the Task Force set the stage to show that UN agencies needed help to facilitate collaboration, that such collaboration was indeed possible, and that it could work. A scant decade earlier, an example already existed to show that when the UN agencies worked together they were able to raise the immunization levels from under 20 percent to 80 percent in only six years.

chapter 16

THE MECTIZAN MIRACLE

In November 1997, I visited a village in Mali and sat with a gathering of village residents on benches that had been pulled together for the meeting. One bench was for blind people. One young man, only thirty-nine years of age, had been blind for twenty-one years. Blind for more than half of his life.

October 21, 1987, may be as important in the history of global health as the breaching of the Berlin Wall was to democracy. That day, a corporation made social need more important than profits—in one of the most unusual coalitions in the public health arena.

The people in that village were very sophisticated about the cause of their blindness, onchocerciasis (river blindness). And they knew, and were grateful, that their children would never have to put up with it. The visit helped those of us who spend time in meetings, thinking about policy or writing papers, to be grounded, to see the actual impact of Merck & Co.'s Mectizan Donation Program, which prevents river blindness. But it was also a chance for the villagers to become connected, to see Merck employees and to know that medicine doesn't just appear in a village by magic. The villagers saw the faces of people who spend their days worrying about schedules and customs, about dosage and packaging, about storage and records. We were reminded that we live in an interdependent world, where it takes the whole world to raise a healthy child.

What led up to that meeting in Mali?

Where does one start? History is always a book that we begin in the middle; however, we must begin someplace. In 1893, onchocerciasis was first described. In 1926, the life cycle of *Onchocerca volvulus*, the parasitic worm that causes it, was finally understood. In 1974, the WHO established the Onchocerciasis Control Program to control the blackflies that transmit this parasite. (That is a story in itself.) Onchocerciasis is the second leading cause of blindness in the world. It also causes debilitating itching.

But the story took a leap forward in 1978, with Merck researcher William Campbell. Campbell, a brilliant parasitologist, has helped develop drugs for some of the neglected diseases of the poorest people in the world. In 2015, he was honored with the Nobel Prize in Physiology or Medicine. In 1978, Campbell went to see Dr. Roy Vagelos, head of Merck Research Labs, with the idea that ivermectin (Mectizan is the brand name), a drug used to prevent heartworm in dogs, might have an effect on onchocerciasis in humans. Campbell's hunch was based on similarities between the two organisms.

However, it would take millions of dollars to determine whether that hunch was correct. Moreover, the potential market for treating humans was small because the area of the world affected by onchocerciasis was extremely poor. Vagelos, with full knowledge of the limited commercial opportunities, decided to approve the proposal.

It is hard to reconstruct the ethos of this company. Its founder's son, George Merck, once declared, "We try never to forget that medicine is for the people. It is not for profits, and if we have remembered that, they have never failed to appear." Add Roy Vagelos to that philosophy, and you have an understanding of what followed.

In February 1981, the University of Dakar conducted the first human tests on whether Mectizan would prevent river blindness in humans. By 1983, the results were so encouraging that phase II studies began. By 1986, phase III studies on 1,200 patients in Ghana and

Liberia had determined optimal dosing. In 1987, papers were filed in France for regulatory approval of the drug for use in humans.

The Task Force Gets Involved

On October 21, 1987, at press conferences in Washington, DC, and Paris, Merck said it would supply Mectizan, for the treatment of river blindness, to everyone who needed it, for as long as necessary, at no charge. That is as important in the history of global health as the breaching of the Berlin Wall was to democracy. John Maynard Keynes once said, "The day is not far off when economic problems will take a back seat to our real problems." He was talking about human relations, behavior, health, and religion. Maybe October 21, 1987, was that day: the moment when a corporation had the audacity to make social need more important than profits—to make a commitment that went beyond what could actually be seen—to treat anyone for free for as long as required.

I wasn't part of that decision. But I am proud to have been part of the rest of the story. After his historic announcement, Vagelos tried to find a way to distribute the drug. He went first to the WHO but found himself overwhelmed by the bureaucracy. He then approached USAID, which was not interested. Merck then came to the Task Force for Child Survival and made the same offer it had made to the WHO and USAID. If Merck gave the drug for free, would we figure out a way to distribute it?

The Task Force agreed and went to work on the big issues. How would it be decided which programs got the drug? How could we determine the adverse effects of the drug? How could it be distributed? What records would be necessary? Could ministries of health be involved in such a way that they would be aware at all times about what was being done in their jurisdictions?

The Task Force and Merck agreed on how the program should be organized. They created the Mectizan Expert Committee, in 1988, to provide a mechanism to make Mectizan available for community use to any applicants who could show they would get the drug to the right people, in the right amounts; that the drug would not be diverted to the marketplace; and that all applications would be approved by the ministry of health of their country so that we could have total transparency with the government. Experts in global health and onchocerciasis were invited to the committee. Merck had members participate in discussions, but they did not vote. The company was serious about donating the drug with no strings attached; this meant allowing outsiders to make decisions. I chaired that committee for twelve years, and the Task Force hired several people to run the program.

I believe in a cause-and-effect world rather than in a world of magic. And yet that doesn't keep me from being filled with awe at the inspirational and even miraculous ingredients of this program. It is unlike any other program in global health.

The birth of the drug involved a soil sample taken from a golf course in Japan, the scientific facilities and managerial abilities of Merck in the United States, the obsession and zeal of Merck researcher Dr. Mohammad Aziz (a tropical disease specialist from Bangladesh, who worked at the WHO before joining Merck), field trials involving people and sites in Africa, and finally, regulatory approval by France. This is a global story.

Drug Safety and Effects

Aside from the miracle of the drug action in clearing microfilaria from the blood is the miraculous unfolding of information on the drug's safety. We were, frankly, afraid. If Mectizan were to have a significant impact, it would have to be given to large numbers of people. We know what happens when you give anything to large numbers of people, no matter how spectacular the overall benefits. There are always adverse effects, which must be weighed against the benefits.

Smallpox vaccine, for example, the most dangerous of all of our vaccines, led to dozens of deaths each year before the disease was eradicated. But the disease was killing millions of people a year (300 million in the twentieth century), and therefore, society was willing to accept the adverse effects of the vaccine. After all, once small-pox was eradicated, the vaccine could be stopped. Polio vaccine has changed the world, and yet some get paralysis from the live vaccine.

So we collectively held our breaths as we worried about (1) how to get large numbers of people to take a medication if they could not expect the benefits for many years, and (2) what to do if serious side effects were apparent at low prevalence.

The first part of this equation proved serendipitously easy. On-chocerciasis causes not only blindness but also an insatiable itching due to the movement of the microfilaria stage of the parasite under the skin of those afflicted. I remember seeing villagers using stones to scratch their skin, the itch was so unbearable. An unexpected effect of Mectizan was it stopped the itching immediately for many people. That, probably more than Mectizan's prevention of blind-ness, led to its avid acceptance in villages.

Originally, our postuse surveillance for possible side effects from the drug called for assistance to be available for seventy-two hours after Mectizan distribution. Gradually, this restriction was lifted, and now we realize Mectizan is one of the safest medications.

A Mectizan Coalition

The miracle of a company donation . . . what is the precedent? The market has its rules, and one of the main ones is that, if there is a problem, the marketplace must always win.

In this case, the management team at Merck, led by Dr. Roy Vage-los, decided social need would win. Revisit the commitment: It was not for as long as Mectizan paid its way in other areas or as long as it fit into their plan; rather, it was for "as long as needed for the treat-ment of onchocerciasis." Forever, if necessary.

Once again, as with the coalition to improve vaccine coverage for children of the world, we saw a magical coalition for Mectizan. It started quite small, including a few people on the Mectizan Expert Committee, the group interested at Merck, and the Onchocerciasis Control Program in West Africa. But it grew. As church-sponsored medical mission groups found they could obtain Mectizan, but only if they applied through the ministry of health to the committee, they worked with governments. Thus, the coalition widened. And soon even the World Bank was involved in developing a fund for Mectizan distribution.

So the gift, in turn, was amplified by a coalition of global organizations, ministries of health, foundations, mission groups, community organizations, and volunteers—all held together by a shared goal rather than by a true organizational structure. It is one of the most unusual coalitions in the history of global health because it doesn't answer to the WHO, UNICEF, or other UN agencies. Part of the impact of Mectizan has been to find new ways of marshaling the forces of the world to improve health.

Mectizan Delivery

Then there is the miracle of Mectizan delivery. We originally hoped to reach 6 million people in six years. We did it in four. When President Carter got involved, the distribution increased rapidly. He would talk to heads of state in Africa, and they would become interested. If they were interested, one could depend on their ministers of health to become interested. Soon the program was reaching 10 million and then 20 million people a year. Each person was at the end of a delivery system that included:

- Applications requiring mail, telephone, fax, and computers
- A secretariat and committee
- Orders placed and sorted in New Jersey
- Tablets bottled, boxed, and shipped from France
- Airlines and customs, clearance and ministries, storage and delivery
- A pipeline of Mectizan flow that branched into thousands of spigots
- Clinics, mobile teams, village workers, drivers, enumerators, and scribes
- Dirt roads, flooded rivers, war and conflict, and every ample barrier that Africa has to offer in reaching its poor

Sightless among Miracles, by R. T. "Skip" Wallen, 1995. Sculpture commissioned by John Moores, founder of the River Blindness Foundation, at the Jimmy Carter Presidential Library and Museum. Photo courtesy Carter Center

Millions of separate stories, with millions of people playing supporting roles—and, yet, despite the odds, it actually worked. We can never become too jaded to simply be amazed at what a coalition can do.

The impact on the microfilaria burden is apparent. Blindness has decreased; transmission rates have been reduced. We can even dream of a time when onchocerciasis is but a memory, a footnote in medical texts and a curiosity in the oral history of a village.

There is a metal sculpture commissioned by John Moores, a businessman and philanthropist who became one of the outstanding warriors in the battle against onchocerciasis. The sculpture shows the familiar figure of a small boy, investing in the future of his African village by guiding a blind man by means of a stick.

The original of this sculpture, *Sightless among Miracles*, sculpted by R. T. "Skip" Wallen, was dedicated in the Merck headquarters' lobby.

I had a chance to comment at that dedication and pointed out that every visitor seeing this sculpture must puzzle over the significance of something that doesn't highlight the cleverest product of Merck, the most profitable product, or the most scientifically advanced example of the company. Instead, it is a monument to human and corporate decency.

The second copy of this sculpture is at the Carter Center, a nongovernmental organization. There it serves as a symbol of hope amid world problems—a statement that individuals, such as President Carter, can make a difference.

The third sculpture is in the lobby of the World Bank. This is perhaps the most unusual setting for this sculpture. It is placed in an institution that frequently is seen as a bank rather than as a health agency. Yet its visitors now see a reminder that the World Bank has mobilized the riches of the world to improve the health of the poorest of the poor.

The fourth copy is at the WHO headquarters in Geneva, the organization that was too bureaucratic to become the distributer of the product.

Jonas Salk used to say that evolution will be what we want it to be, and that the only successful way to predict the future is to invent it. The Mectizan Donation Program invented the future by not being tied to historical shackles.

History would never have given us a reason to believe that a pharmaceutical company would give a major amount of a drug free . . . forever.

History could not have predicted a coalition that would be so broad, so committed, so productive.

History would not have given us great confidence that communities would manage their own distribution program.

And history certainly would not have led us to results better than our most optimistic predictions.

When I talked to the program participants at the tenth anniversary, I mentioned Stacey King, who played his first year in professional basketball for the Chicago Bulls. He had a night when he made only a single point. Michael Jordan made sixty-nine points that night.

When a reporter asked King to comment on his performance he said, "I will always remember this as the night that I combined with Michael Jordan for seventy points."

And we will say, *This was the time that we each did so little, and yet we combined for a victory over a scourge, a plague which afflicted the neediest.*

Would this have happened without the Bellagio creation of the Task Force? It is impossible to know. But the experience with a coalition outside of the UN agencies gave Merck the courage to approach the Task Force and gave us the courage to try an entirely different way of providing for the product's distribution.

chapter 17
THE TASK FORCE FOR GLOBAL HEALTH

Following the Summit for Children, the Task Force changed its name to the Task Force for Child Survival and Development in 1991. The name change reflected an expanding agenda, which had moved far beyond the original objective of increasing immunization coverage.

Then serendipity struck once again. A Mectizan Expert Committee meeting was being held in France, the country that packaged and shipped all of the Mectizan used for onchocerciasis. It was a routine meeting until Thursday afternoon, when Dr. Eric Ottesen, a tropical disease specialist at the World Health Organization (WHO), reported on a study that combined Mectizan and Albendazole (used to treat a variety of parasitic infestations) to observe the effects on persons with yet another tropical infection, lymphatic filiariasis. This last disease is better known as elephantiasis and is characterized by swelling, especially of the legs and scrotum. The use of both drugs led to an unexpected positive effect: it reduced the parasitic burden in patients and reduced transmission of parasites to others.

Albendazole was produced by SmithKline Beecham, Dr. Ottesen reported. The group brainstormed to see whether anyone knew a person in that company at a high-enough level to OK providing free Albendazole for an expansion of the drug-combination studies and possibly a program to prevent lymphatic filiariasis. No one did, but the group remained highly energized by the thought of a new tool for a neglected disease of the world. The conversations continued at dinner.

At 10 a.m. the next day, I was chairing the meeting when a person slipped a note in front of me to say that President Carter was on the phone. Would I take the call? We broke for coffee, and I went to an office to take the call.

President Carter said it was 5 a.m. in Atlanta, but he was so excited that he wanted to talk to me. He asked whether the name Jan Leschly meant anything to me. No, I responded. President Carter said he had had dinner with him the night before in Washington, DC, and that Leschly mentioned how impressed he was with Merck's gift of supplying Mectizan free to those afflicted with onchocerciasis. Not only was this donation helpful to the world, Leschly noted, it was also helpful to Merck because the gift inspired such staff loyalty. People like to work for a company that demonstrates social concern.

I asked President Carter what Leschly's position was. President Carter replied that Leschly was the CEO of SmithKline Beecham and that he was asking President Carter for ideas on what his company might do that would be similar to Merck's contribution. By the end of the day, President Carter had a commitment for Albendazole.

There were many steps to be taken. Could two competing pharmaceutical companies work together to provide their drugs? The findings had to be confirmed and expanded. Studies were required to detect adverse effects in people receiving both drugs. And experience was required to see whether delivery techniques could be developed that would be acceptable to people in areas affected by lymphatic filariasis. But that day was the beginning of the Global Lymphatic Filiariasis Program.

It took several years to iron out the problems to make it possible for the two corporations to actually institute a joint program. The need to ensure that the combination of the two drugs had no adverse effects on recipients was especially troublesome. Each company, quite correctly, felt that it had conducted studies to show that its drug, given alone, was safe. Why did the company need to give additional resources to test the effect of another company's drug added to theirs?

The WHO finally called for a meeting in Amsterdam to find a way around this dilemma. I was asked to chair the meeting, and a solution was quickly achieved. The example of immunization became the way forward. Vaccines had gone through phase 1, phase 2, and phase 3 trials before being supported by the WHO. However, no vaccine company had been forced to demonstrate what would happen if another vaccine was added and administered simultaneously. Moreover, there were programs in Africa administering smallpox, measles, DPT, and polio vaccines to the same child at the same visit. In some areas yellow fever vaccine was also given. How did that happen? The CDC, WHO, and others conducted the necessary vaccination-combination studies because it was to the benefit of global health to be able to do this. The companies were not asked to guarantee the safety of combinations.

This, then, became the answer for Mectizan and Albendazole. The WHO needed to supervise and develop such studies. And the program has prospered. Finally, in 1998, the Global Alliance to Eliminate Lymphatic Filariasis was formed with a remarkable humanitarian partnership between Merck and SmithKline Beecham.

In 2015, studies provided yet another advance. They showed that when Mectizan and Albendazole were combined with DEC (a synthetic derivative of piperazine, also used as an anthelmintic drug in treating filariasis) parasite reduction was accelerated and transmission was reduced more than with any single- or double-drug program. Global health continues to become more exciting with each year.

Expansion at the End of the Millennium

During the 1990s, the Task Force rapidly expanded into other programs. In 1992, the Task Force started a program called All Kids Count, funded by the Robert Wood Johnson Foundation and other foundations to help develop community-based immunization registries in the United States. Now called immunization systems, these registries consolidate a child's immunizations into one record, regardless of where he or she received the vaccines.

The public health community had naively assumed that providing information on the need for immunization and putting up road signs that said, for example, "Be Wise, Immunize" would have an impact. Careful evaluation found these approaches did nothing. Parents thought that, by taking their children to the pediatrician, their child's vaccine needs were being provided. Meanwhile, pediatricians assumed their systems were working; if asked about the level of immunization in their practice, they would generally assume it was about 90 percent. A review of their records would often show the true immunization status to be as low as 60 percent or 65 percent.

Faced with such results, pediatricians would quickly move to correct the situation. Therefore, a record system that could daily show them, on their computer screen, the immunization level for each vaccine in their practice was a practical way for them to correct the shortfall. This program has improved record keeping, identified pockets of unimmunized children, and avoided duplicate vaccinations.

The Task Force became involved in many activities that could improve global health. Often it would organize meetings for government, the UN, or private groups. It eventually changed names again, in 2009, this time to the Task Force for Global Health. A listing of some of its activities demonstrates its importance.

In 1994, the Task Force studied the possibilities of developing a foundation that could assist the CDC but remain a nonprofit organization separate from the CDC. A plan was developed that led to the establishment, by Congress, of the CDC Foundation in 1995. In its first twenty years, the foundation has launched more than 700 projects globally while providing more than $600 million to CDC programs.

The next year, the Task Force partnered with the WHO, the CDC, and Rotary International to help build the Global Polio Eradication Laboratory Network. Walter Dowdle, formerly the director of the Center for Infectious Diseases at the CDC, helped to set up labs and train personnel around the world to isolate and characterize polio strains as they were recovered from outbreaks.

Continued

- The Task Force partnered with the WHO, US agencies, and the Bill & Melinda Gates Foundation to establish the Poliovirus Antiviral Drugs Initiative. This program attempts to develop alternative approaches to treating people who excrete poliovirus over long periods of time because of an immunologic defect. Development of a drug would also provide an additional tool in managing polio outbreaks.
- The Lymphatic Filariasis Support Center joined the Task Force with a focus on monitoring, evaluating, and providing advocacy for the global efforts to reduce the toll of this crippling affliction.
- The National Viral Hepatitis Roundtable joined the Task Force. This coalition of advocacy organizations, government agencies, insurers, and others is dedicated to developing and implementing a national strategy to eliminate viral hepatitis.
- TEPHINET (Training Programs in Epidemiology and Public Health Interventions Network), a program supported by CDC to strengthen international public health, has become a program of the Task Force.
- The International Trachoma Initiative (ITI) also became a program of the Task Force. By 2009, ITI had facilitated efforts to eliminate trachoma through support for 352,000 sight-saving surgeries and more than 77 million Zithromax treatments in fifteen countries.

*MH Bornstein, L Davidson, CLM Keyes, KA Moore, editors. *Well-Being: Positive Development across the Life Course,* Crosscurrents in Contemporary Psychology Series (New York: Psychology Press, 2003).

In 1996, the Task Force and the Carter Center sponsored Children First: A Global Forum, which brought together representatives from sixty-six countries to create a model for change that would improve the lives of children. The model focused on health, education, safety, protection, and economic security.

In 1999, Dr. Mark Rosenberg became the executive director of the Task Force. Under his leadership, a formidable list of global and domestic programs was instituted (see box). Many involved collabora-

tions between multiple partners. Indeed, the Task Force began research on encouraging coalitions and collaboration in global health,
an effort made possible with support from the Bill & Melinda Gates
Foundation, the Rockefeller Foundation, and the CDC. In 2010,
Dr. Rosenberg and others at the Task Force published *Real Collaboration: What It Takes for Global Health to Succeed* (1).

In 2016, David Ross became director, after sixteen year as director
of the Task Force's Public Health Informatics Institute and its prede-
cessor, All Kids Count.

The work of the Task Force has become more remarkable every
year. In 2013, the *Chronicle of Philanthropy* listed the organization
as the fourth most successful in the nation in its ability to raise resources (2). By 2010, the figure for such resources was $1.14 billion;
most of this was in the form of drug donations from a variety of
corporations, which went toward programs for neglected diseases
in Africa, Asia, and the Americas. By 2012, the Task Force had raised
$1.656 billion in a single year (2).

Originally formed to accelerate progress in global immunizations, the Task Force has become a superb vehicle for global health
delivery programs of many kinds.

chapter 18

LESSONS

The three-day meeting in March 1984 at the Rockefeller Center in Bellagio, resulted in changes in global health that persist thirty years later, often without the knowledge of the people now involved in those programs. The group approved the creation of a Task Force for Child Survival, to help facilitate immunization activities conducted by global and bilateral groups.

The original objective of the WHO and UNICEF to improve global immunization coverage was achieved. Immunization rates that were as low as 14 percent for measles in 1984 improved dramatically in six years to the point that Jim Grant, executive director of UNICEF, announced at the Summit for Children on September 30, 1990, that 80 percent of children in the world had received at least one vaccine.

During that time, UNICEF and the WHO alone received $1 billion in immunization resources. A new level of resource support had been established.

In addition, a number of movements were started. In March 1988, Rafe Henderson presented to the assembled Bellagio III meeting in Talloires, France, a list of health objectives that the WHO deemed worthy targets for the year 2000. As stated earlier, this was the first time that global health goals had actually been written up. The delegates approved the list, and it was published (1).

Three efforts continue with major impact thirty years later. One of these is the Global Alliance for Vaccines and Immunizations (GAVI). In six short years in the 1980s, the Task Force demonstrated that global programs could improve immunization coverage if they combined efforts. Established global health agencies worked better when facilitation from the outside was provided. However, the effort fell apart with new leadership in both UNICEF and the WHO in the 1990s.

With the financial support of the Bill & Melinda Gates Foundation, a mechanism for improving vaccine coverage, adding new and expensive vaccines for poor countries, speeding up the development of vaccines, and improving delivery mechanisms encouraged agencies to once again collaborate for a desired goal. GAVI has stability that should ensure a solid global immunization future and demonstrates anew the value of outside organizations to support the WHO and UNICEF.

The second of these efforts, the Mectizan Donation Program for onchocerciasis, has now passed the quarter-century mark with a record of more than 1 billion treatments donated by Merck & Co. It is not only a stunning outcome of the 1984 Bellagio meeting, but it also may be the most unique of all global health programs. The structure is simply a coalition held together by an expert committee and a shared objective, with no global superstructure.

The third major outcome is the evolution of the Task Force for Child Survival into the Task Force for Child Survival and Development and then into the Task Force for Global Health, with its impressive involvement in a myriad of activities and its prodigious fund-raising capabilities (2). It demonstrates the vital contributions of a nonprofit organization. The organizers of the Bellagio conference in March 1984 could not have foreseen the long-term benefits of their discussions and decisions.

Lessons Learned

An important realization in this saga is the fragility and limitations of UN organizations. Seven decades after the creation of the

WHO (and fourteen other UN agencies), we realize there is no substitute. If we didn't have a WHO, we would need to develop one. And yet it can be so dysfunctional that it at times throws us into despair. The recent Ebola outbreak again reminded us that we have not created and funded an organization capable of protecting us.

It has many things going against it. When the WHO was created, the United States insisted on strong regional offices to protect the very strong Pan American Health Organization. But the result has been a system that allows regional directors great power and the ability to influence their elections and reelections. Thus, Geneva is often unable to provide global leadership.

The idea of a board of directors that consists of all ministers of health is mind-boggling. To get an agreement from a group that turns over so fast that many attend the annual meetings for two or three years, only to be replaced, strains credibility. Continuity is difficult. No CEO would agree to run a company with that kind of board of directors. The need for national balance makes it difficult not only to get the best people in the world but also to have bold decision making if employees fear losing such good positions.

With good leadership some of these problems can be mitigated, but with poor leadership, the inherent problems become even more oppressive. Add to this the annual berating of the organization by member states to reduce its budget. That WHO leaders have been able to provide so many benefits to the health of the world is commendable. But they could have done much more with better structures, support, and adequate funding.

- -
Everything requires a coalition. Nothing is done by a single individual.
- -

So the first lesson is the need to get agency heads to step back and collectively ask what has been learned about UN agencies in seven decades and how could they be better organized at this point to truly serve the needs of the world?

A second lesson is that it is possible to enlist the help of an outside group, such as the Task Force for Child Survival or GAVI, to facilitate a better result than might come from the agencies alone.

A third lesson is that everything requires a coalition. Nothing is done by a single individual. And there are lessons on what makes a coalition successful. The lessons include the fact that the heads of the components, whether two groups or many, must want the coalition to work. It can't be organized at lower levels in the organization and be fruitful if the leaders are not invested. For one shining six-year period, there was an agreement and a desire for success by the heads of the WHO, UNICEF, United Nations Development Programme, and the World Bank, all facilitated by the Rockefeller Foundation. This was enough time to accelerate the global program and push immunization levels to 80 percent. As important as the UN agencies are, they were made even better by an outside group's facilitating their activities. GAVI is now serving that purpose. Perhaps one of the major seventy-year lessons might be how best to use outside organizations to help UN agencies to excel.

The beginning of the end was seen when a new director-general of the WHO, Dr. Nakajima, was elected in 1988. Collaboration was not his style. The momentum of the global group was able to continue for a few years more, however. Then the appointment of a new executive director of UNICEF, Carol Bellamy, in 1995, sealed the fate of the coalition, and immunization programs stagnated until revived by Bill and Melinda Gates.

Another lesson was the need for clear definitions of success. Originally, it was improved immunization coverage, but that was not specific enough. When Jim Grant defined it as 80 percent coverage, the last mile became clear. Later, a second target of polio eradication became another rallying point for immunization programs.

A fifth lesson was to deliberately take on the function of problem solving. A prime objective of core meetings was to understand the barriers to improved coverage and to systematically reduce them. Eliciting the ideas of field staff as to the major barriers that required research and solutions was an important part of understanding what could be done.

A sixth lesson was to emphasize communications. Attempts were made through quarterly meetings of the Task Force core group, global meetings at approximately two-year intervals, a newsletter

(*World Immunization News*), and constant communications from the
WHO and UNICEF to the field, to keep everyone informed on immunization events.

For a shining six-year period, there was agreement and a desire for
success by the heads of the WHO, UNICEF, United Nations Development Programme, and the World Bank, all facilitated by the
Rockefeller Foundation. This was enough time to accelerate the global
program and push immunization levels to 80 percent.

A seventh lesson concerned the importance of political leadership. The dynamism of Jim Grant and Halfdan Mahler and their
deliberate involvement of heads of state were crucial elements in
motivating ministers of health and ministers of finance. Every public health decision eventually rests on a political decision to make
the public health decision workable. The fact that seventy-one
heads of state attended the Summit for Children on September 30,
1990, is a reflection of the work agency heads did to enlist political
support.

The smallpox eradication lessons were also relevant, namely:

- Success is not an accident. It requires work.
- Know the truth. It is the only way to improve.
- Systematically improve the tools, the organization, and the evaluation of the program.
- Trust is the glue that holds coalitions together, and it is earned,
  not purchased.
- Social will is as necessary as political will.
- Management is the key to success. Knowledge can be obtained
  in many ways, but whether that knowledge changes health is a
  matter of management.
- Think long-term. Our bosses are really the people to be born in
  the future, and they are totally dependent on the decisions we
  now make. They don't know that they have given us their proxy
  vote to create the world in which they will live.
- Tenacity and optimism are of the highest value.

- Find deficiencies and correct them.
- It is possible to plan a rational future.

An enduring lesson is that there are many ways to structure organizations, but the UN and global agencies have become somewhat homogeneous, to their detriment. In 1991, Newton Bowles of UNICEF attempted to identify the characteristics of the Task Force that made it productive and unique. His list included:

1. Its *mandate* comes directly from agency heads. The Task Force depends on their personal interest and support.
2. During most of its lifetime, its *focus* has been on clear and relatively simple objectives.
3. As an *ad hoc* arrangement, it is relatively nonthreatening to vested interests.
4. It is *informal*.
5. It is *small*.
6. It is *professional*.
7. It has enjoyed a high degree of *continuity* in membership.
8. It has had *outstanding staff support and leadership* in Atlanta.
9. It meets in a *collegial, trusting atmosphere,* allowing free discussion of serious and sensitive matters.
10. *Networking* internationally is achieved because members serve in many related activities.
11. It has been *flexible and adaptive* in what it does.
12. Members believe in what they are doing. They have *commitment* and *enthusiasm* (3).

Words often fail to describe emotions. There is no way to totally convey the joy of being a grandparent, for instance, until one experiences grandparenthood. Nor is there a way to convey the terror of being poverty-stricken until you have no way to feed your child. And there is no way to adequately prepare for the shock of a cancer diagnosis until you are told you have cancer.

Likewise, empathy goes only so far in imagining what it is like to have measles in an African village, when you are already malnourished, anemic because of hookworms, and you harbor schistosomiasis, dracunculiasis, filariasis, and malaria. Or if you are a mother trying to comfort that child. Just as there is no way for that mother to totally appreciate her child's *not* having measles because of unseen hands that somehow got protective vaccine from a pharmaceutical house through countless difficulties to her child's immune system. And there is no way for the owners of those unseen hands to know what joy they have allowed to exist in villages and slums around the world. Globalism has its price, but it also has its benefits.

Imagine being an independent spirit, farming in West Africa, proud of providing food for your family, only to have sight fade in your forties and then disappear totally when you are fifty. Now you are reduced to dependency, as a child leads you around the village. And even blindness is not the whole picture of river blindness; intense itching makes the suffering even greater.

But indifference is not destiny. And global health coalitions can change what has been the fate of many poor people in villages around the world. As already highlighted, UNICEF used to distribute a poster of Selamawit, the Ethiopian child, who, when asked what she wanted to be when she grew up, said, "Alive!" The agencies involved in the programs described here made that wish a reality for millions of children. That reality is not short-lived. It ripples on forever.

ACKNOWLEDGMENTS

It is incredibly difficult to write a book, and it requires more than a village. There are all the people who made the work possible plus those who made the book possible. Numerous people at the Centers for Disease Control and Prevention supported the work and this publication. James Mason, CDC director, provided support for me as the Task Force for Child Survival was forming. Special thanks to workers in the CDC's immunization program who provided constant help, especially Alan Hinman, Walt Orenstein, Walter Dowdle, Steve Cochi, and a host of others.

The primary support agencies worked harmoniously to make this a success. At UNICEF, Jim Grant found ways to support the work financially and through staff. Newton Bowles provided wisdom, humor, and perspective. Steve Joseph initially, and Terrel Hill later, provided representation and enormous efforts to coordinate with other agencies and countries. The World Health Organization support started with Halfdan Mahler, but the primary representative to coordinate work around the world was Rafe Henderson. He never failed to attend quarterly meetings or to carry out a host of requests that would result from those meetings. The United Nations Development Programme was so ably represented by Tim Rothermel, who used his extensive experience to make things happen. At the World Bank, a slow start was remedied when Tony Measham became the representative and found ways to improve this international organization's support. At the Rockefeller Foundation, Ken Warren, an irrepressible person with ideas and admonitions, made sure the foundation did not lose interest.

The Task Force could have faltered without the support of Emory University. With the Task Force's small budget, drawing up regulations for travel, communications, personnel and benefits, and the like was just not possible. Fortunately, the president of Emory, Jim

Laney, understood the importance of the Task Force, if it succeeded. He agreed to let us contract for all of the support services and agreed that I could answer to him directly. These were invaluable gifts.

Unforeseen when we started, the assistance of Merck & Co. was the beginning of an entirely new chapter in global health with the Mectizan Donation Program. So many were involved, but Roy Vagelos, the CEO of Merck, made it all possible. Bill Campbell provided the scientific impetus for discovering the power of Mectizan. Ken Brown provided medical expertise; plus, having worked in Africa, he had an idea of what might work in the field. Charlie Fettig served as a Merck representative with enormous experience on how the company works and what it could do. The daily work of getting orders sent to numerous countries and solving internal program problems and relationships with other groups was so ably handled by Brenda Colatrella. An unknown number of employees quietly worked behind the scene.

In addition, the work was possible because of literally hundreds of agencies, nongovernmental organizations, governments, universities, missionaries, and supporters from all walks of life. Mark Rosenberg, as director of the Task Force beginning in 1999, not only helped to strengthen and expand the Mectizan program but also used the experience to encourage other companies to support global health efforts by donating products for a host of neglected diseases that affect poor countries.

Current Task Force director David Ross undertook the mission of locating and reproducing twenty-five-year-old visuals. Special thanks to Joni Lawrence for locating the original copy of the Selamawit poster and to Poul Olson for taking a photo of it for us.

The writing itself was made possible by a short period in residence at the Rockefeller Center in Bellagio, Italy. Staff were helpful in providing support, interest, solutions to problems, and an ideal environment. Mary Hilpertshauser at the CDC's Sencer Museum helped secure photographs. My wife, Paula, provided a diagnostic and therapeutic touch, changing thoughts and phrases that she understood, as the result of the language that develops between spouses after many decades, but that would have made no sense to others.

Thanks to Johns Hopkins University Press for their willingness to consider this publication, and especially to Robin W. Coleman, who took a personal interest in reading and offering suggestions. His discussions with unknown reviewers made the book better and more understandable. Thanks also to Isla Hamilton-Short and Sahara Clement for managing the book's visuals.

Thanks beyond measure to Anne Mather, who understands how to untangle language and make it more accurate. She also has the special patience required to learn the rules imposed by those who might be willing to take a chance on publishing. She understands the mechanics of editing but also how nuanced writing can be. Finally, she has an instinct for headings and reorganization of ideas. I am immensely grateful for her help. Without her there would be no book.

APPENDIX A

THE ROCKEFELLER FOUNDATION

Select the name of any person in America and a chapter could be written on the influence the Rockefeller Foundation has had on that person.

I take myself as an example. My career in global health was aided by a gift from the Rockefellers (even before the foundation was formed) to the London School of Hygiene and Tropical Medicine. I went there for briefings in 1965 before working in Africa and again on sabbatical in 1992.

Another example: Everyone in medicine and public health has been influenced by the work of Abraham Flexner. Flexner was first sponsored by the Carnegie Foundation, after the president of the foundation, Henry Pritchett, read Flexner's critiques on education programs and hired him to investigate professional education programs. Flexner published his report on medical education in 1910, before the Rockefeller Foundation started.

When the foundation began, its strong interest in medical education led to sponsorship of Flexner and ultimately a report on public health education. This, in turn, resulted in the first school of public health in the United States at Johns Hopkins University. When I applied to the Harvard School of Public Health, some twenty programs had been inspired by that first school. That number has subsequently doubled.

In the early twentieth century, yellow fever was one of the most frightening diseases in the world. The Rockefeller Foundation became interested in the problem, and after World War I, the foundation expanded yellow fever work to Africa by creating a laboratory near Lagos, Nigeria. It was to be both productive and tragic. One member of the group, Adrian Stokes, a pathology professor from London, was the first victim of yellow fever. The next was Hideyo Noguchi, a physician from Japan who worked at the Rockefeller Institute. His autopsy was conducted by William Young, who also died of yellow fever. Global health work was high risk at that time. Even then global health workers were unrelenting optimists.

Then a series of breakthroughs permitted the isolation and then transport of a virus in a frozen state to New York. Work at the Rockefeller Institute with cell cultures led to the development of the 17D yellow fever vaccine by Max Theiler. Theiler, from South Africa, whom the Rockefeller Foundation hired in 1930 from Harvard, received a Nobel Prize for his work in 1951. This vaccine, still in use, has made work in Africa safer.

In the early 1930s, the Rockefeller Foundation had agreed to new facilities for research at the American University in Beirut. Edward Turner, a new graduate in physiology from the University of Chicago, arrived in Beirut as an assistant professor of physiology. He felt inadequately prepared, so the Rockefeller Foundation provided a fellowship for him to attend medical school at the University of Pennsylvania. He returned to Beirut to head the Department of Medicine.

Returning to the United States in 1936, Turner was met at the ship by Alan Gregg from the Rockefeller Foundation, who persuaded him to take over the Department of Medicine at Meharry Medical College in Nashville. He became the third president of Meharry two years later.

After eight years, Turner entered private practice only to receive four offers for medical school deanships. He was not tempted except by an offer from the University of Washington for a free hand in starting a new medical school. He visited in September 1945, and the challenge plus the commitments of the University of Washington were so impressive that he immediately accepted. Within three years, he had constructed the first medical school building on the lower campus golf course. To take over a golf course requires considerable political skill. That golf course eventually became the home of the sprawling University of Washington medical complex. I benefited from the Rockefeller investment when I began classes there nine years after the first building was completed.

One of the doctors who was influential in starting the school, Dr. Alfred Strauss, graduated from the University of Washington in 1904. He was given the Alumnus Summa Laude Dignatus Award in 1951 for his work in founding the school and for support of the university's sports program. While living in Chicago, he hosted the University of Washington crew team on their way to Berlin to win the Olympic Gold Medal in 1936. He spent his early years in Colville, Washington, the small town where I graduated from high school many years later.

During medical school, a classmate, Robert Eelkema, gave me *An American Doctor's Odyssey: Adventures in Forty-Five Countries,* by Victor Heiser (1). It recounts his experiences in dozens of countries, much of the work sponsored by Rockefeller. It gave me glimpses of what was possible in global health.

In the early 1940s, the foundation provided a fellowship for a physician in India to study public health. That man later became the commissioner of health for Delhi. His son, Mahendra Dutta, followed in his footsteps, worked on smallpox eradication, and later also became the commissioner of health for Delhi. His grandson, Umesh Parasher, followed the family tradition and went into public health. He is now an accomplished scientist at the CDC in

Atlanta. Three generations sponsored by one Rockefeller fellowship, and I have been privileged to work with the second and third generations of that investment.

As Kurt Vonnegut said, "And so it goes." The list of Rockefeller influences on my life continued. I had the opportunity to work with Norman Borlaug, another Nobel laureate. With foundation help, he promoted the Green Revolution in Southeast Asia. The many interactions I have had with the Rockefeller Foundation include serving on its board, working with countless staff and foundation projects over the years, and involvement with the Task Force for Child Survival. A Rockefeller writing fellowship at Bellagio in 2013 allowed me to write this book.

APPENDIX B

WORLD DECLARATION ON THE SURVIVAL, PROTECTION AND
DEVELOPMENT OF CHILDREN

Agreed to at the World Summit for Children on 30 September 1990, New York

1. We have gathered at the World Summit for Children to undertake a joint commitment and to make an urgent universal appeal—to give every child a better future.
2. The children of the world are innocent, vulnerable and dependent . . . They are also curious, active and full of hope. Their time should be one of joy and peace, of playing, learning and growing. Their future should be shaped in harmony and co-operation. Their lives should mature, as they broaden their perspectives and gain new experiences.
3. But for many children, the reality of childhood is altogether different.

The challenge
4. Each day, countless children around the world are exposed to dangers that hamper their growth and development. They suffer immensely as casualties of war and violence; as victims of racial discrimination, apartheid, aggression, foreign occupation and annexation; as refugees and displaced children, forced to abandon their homes and their roots; as disabled; or as victims of neglect, cruelty and exploitation.
5. Each day, millions of children suffer from the scourges of poverty and economic crisis—from hunger and homelessness, from epidemics and illiteracy, from degradation of the environment. They suffer from the grave effects of the problems of external indebtedness and also from the lack of sustained and sustainable growth in many developing countries, particularly the least developed ones.
6. Each day, 40,000 children die from malnutrition and disease, including acquired immunodeficiency syndrome (AIDS), from the lack of clean water and inadequate sanitation and from the effects of the drug problem.
7. These are challenges that we, as political leaders, must meet.

The opportunity
8. Together, our nations have the means and the knowledge to protect the lives and to diminish enormously the suffering of children, to promote the full development of their human potential and to make them aware of their needs, rights and opportunities.

133

The Convention on the Rights of the Child [https:www.unicef.org/crc] provides a new opportunity to make respect for children's rights and welfare truly universal.

9. Recent improvements in the international political climate can facilitate this task. Through international co-operation and solidarity it should now be possible to achieve concrete results in many fields—to revitalize economic growth and development, to protect the environment, to prevent the spread of fatal and crippling diseases and to achieve greater social and economic justice. The current moves towards disarmament also mean that significant resources could be released for purposes other than military ones. Improving the well-being of children must be a very high priority when these resources are reallocated.

The task

10. Enhancement of children's health and nutrition is a first duty, and also a task for which solutions are now within reach. The lives of tens of thousands of boys and girls can be saved every day, because the causes of their death are readily preventable. Child and infant mortality is unacceptably high in many parts of the world but can be lowered dramatically with means that are already known and easily accessible.

11. Further attention, care and support should be accorded to disabled children, as well as to other children in very difficult circumstances.

12. Strengthening the role of women in general and ensuring their equal rights will be to the advantage of the world's children. Girls must be given equal treatment and opportunities from the very beginning.

13. At present, over 100 million children are without basic schooling, and two-thirds of them are girls. The provision of basic education and literacy for all are among the most important contributions that can be made to the development of the world's children.

14. Half a million mothers die each year from causes related to childbirth. Safe motherhood must be promoted in all possible ways. Emphasis must be placed on responsible planning of family size and on child spacing. The family, as a fundamental group and natural environment for the growth and well-being of children, should be given all necessary protection and assistance.

15. All children must be given the chance to find their identity and realize their worth in a safe and supportive environment, through families and other care-givers committed to their welfare. They must be prepared for responsible life in a free society. They should, from their early years, be encouraged to participate in the cultural life of their societies.

16. Economic conditions will continue to influence greatly the fate of children, especially in developing nations. For the sake of the future of all children, it is urgently necessary to ensure or reactivate sustained and sustainable economic growth and development in all countries and also to continue to give urgent attention to an early, broad and durable solution to the external debt problems facing developing debtor countries.

17. These tasks require a continued and concerted effort by all nations, through national action and international co-operation.

The commitment

18. The well-being of children requires political action at the highest level. We are determined to take that action.

19. We ourselves hereby make a solemn commitment to give high priority to the rights of children, to their survival and to their protection and development. This will also ensure the well-being of all societies.

20. We have agreed that we will act together, in international co-operation, as well as in our respective countries. We now commit ourselves to the following 10-point programme to protect the rights of children and to improve their lives:

(1) We will work to promote earliest possible ratification and implementation of the Convention on the Rights of the Child. Programmes to encourage information about children's rights should be launched world-wide, taking into account the distinct cultural and social values in different countries.

(2) We will work for a solid effort of national and international action to enhance children's health, to promote pre-natal care and to lower infant and child mortality in all countries and among all peoples. We will promote the provision of clean water in all communities for all their children, as well as universal access to sanitation.

(3) We will work for optimal growth and development in childhood, through measures to eradicate hunger, malnutrition and famine, and thus to relieve millions of children of tragic sufferings in a world that has the means to feed all its citizens.

(4) We will work to strengthen the role and status of women. We will promote responsible planning of family size, child spacing, breastfeeding and safe motherhood.

(5) We will work for respect for the role of the family in providing for children and will support the efforts of parents, other care-givers and communities to nurture and care for children, from the earliest stages of

childhood through adolescence. We also recognize the special needs of children who are separated from their families.

(6) We will work for programmes that reduce illiteracy and provide educational opportunities for all children, irrespective of their background and gender; that prepare children for productive employment and lifelong learning opportunities, i.e. through vocational training; and that enable children to grow to adulthood within a supportive and nurturing cultural and social context.

(7) We will work to ameliorate the plight of millions of children who live under especially difficult circumstances—as victims of apartheid and foreign occupation; orphans and street children and children of migrant workers; the displaced children and victims of natural and man-made disasters; the disabled and the abused, the socially disadvantaged and the exploited. Refugee children must be helped to find new roots in life. We will work for special protection of the working child and for the abolition of illegal child labour. We will do our best to ensure that children are not drawn into becoming victims of the scourge of illicit drugs.

(8) We will work carefully to protect children from the scourge of war and to take measures to prevent further armed conflicts, in order to give children everywhere a peaceful and secure future. We will promote the values of peace, understanding and dialogue in the education of children. The essential needs of children and families must be protected even in times of war and in violence-ridden areas. We ask that periods of tranquillity and special relief corridors be observed for the benefit of children, where war and violence are still taking place.

(9) We will work for common measures for the protection of the environment, at all levels, so that all children can enjoy a safer and healthier future.

(10) We will work for a global attack on poverty, which would have immediate benefits for children's welfare. The vulnerability and special needs of the children of the developing countries, and in particular the least developed ones, deserve priority. But growth and development need promotion in all States, through national action and international cooperation. That calls for transfers of appropriate additional resources to developing countries as well as improved terms of trade, further trade liberalization and measures for debt relief. It also implies structural adjustments that promote world economic growth, particularly in developing countries, while ensuring the well-being of the most vulnerable sectors of the populations, in particular the children.

The next steps

21. The World Summit for Children has presented us with a challenge to take action. We have agreed to take up that challenge.

22. Among the partnerships we seek, we turn especially to children themselves. We appeal to them to participate in this effort.

23. We also seek the support of the United Nations system, as well as other international and regional organizations, in the universal effort to promote the well-being of children. We ask for greater involvement on the part of non-governmental organizations, in complementing national efforts and joint international action in this field.

24. We have decided to adopt and implement a Plan of Action, as a framework for more specific national and international undertakings. We appeal to all our colleagues to endorse that Plan. We are prepared to make available the resources to meet these commitments, as part of the priorities of our national plans.

25. We do this not only for the present generation, but for all generations to come. There can be no task nobler than giving every child a better future.

REFERENCES

Introduction
1. Foege WH. House on fire: The fight to eradicate smallpox. Berkeley: University of California Press; 2011.

Chapter 1. The Plot
1. An uneven recovery for America's biggest charities. News and Analysis. Chronicle of Philanthropy, October 20, 2013. The Philanthropy 400 was compiled by EC Grovum, S Frostenson, M Lopez-Rivera, and S Speicher.

Chapter 4. How Productive Coalitions Begin
1. Henderson RH. Impossible! Immunizing the children of the world. Hyderabad: Orient Blackswan; 2016.

Chapter 5. Bellagio, March 1984
1. Protecting the world's children: Vaccines and immunizations within primary health care. Conference report. New York: The Rockefeller Foundation; 1984.
2. Bowles N. The Task Force for Child Survival and Development—hope as energy: An experiment 1984-1998. New York: United Nations; 1998.

Chapter 7. Heads of State Give Vaccinations in Colombia
1. Henderson RH. Impossible! Immunizing the children of the world. Hyderabad: Orient Blackswan; 2016.
2. Bowles N. The Task Force for Child Survival and Development—hope as energy: An experiment 1984-1998. New York: United Nations; 1998.

Chapter 8. Bellagio II in Cartagena, October 1985
1. Protecting the world's children: "Bellagio II" at Cartagena, Colombia, October 1985. Conference report. Atlanta: The Task Force for Child Survival; New York: The Rockefeller Foundation; 1986.

Chapter 10. Bellagio III in Talloires, France, March 1988
1. Protecting the world's children: An agenda for the 1990s. Tufts University European Center, Talloires, France, March 10-12, 1988. Conference report. Atlanta: The Task Force for Child Survival; 1988.

2. Henderson RH. Impossible! Immunizing the children of the world. Hyderabad: Orient Blackswan; 2016.
3. Protecting the world's children: A call for action. Fourth International Child Survival Conference, Bangkok, Thailand, March 1-3, 1990. Conference report. Atlanta: Task Force for Child Survival; 1990:20.

Chapter 12. Bangkok's Messages for World Leaders
1. Protecting the world's children: A call for action. Fourth International Child Survival Conference, Bangkok, Thailand, March 1-3, 1990. Conference report. Atlanta: Task Force for Child Survival; 1990.
2. Protecting the world's children: A call for action. Fourth International Child Survival Conference, Bangkok, Thailand, March 1-3, 1990. Conference proceedings. New York: The Rockefeller Foundation; 1990.
3. Report from the Task Force including John Bennett's statistical data on increased survival linked to reduced population growth. In: Protecting the world's children; 1990: 14-43.
4. UNICEF. The state of the world's children. New York: UNICEF; 1989.
5. Affirmation of Bangkok. In: Protecting the world's children; 1990:1-2.
6. Facts for life. New York: UNICEF, WHO, UNESCO, UNFPA, UNDP, UNAIDS, WFP, and the World Bank; 1989.

Chapter 13. The Summit for Children
1. UNICEF. State of the world's children, 1991. Oxford: Oxford University Press and UNICEF; 1991.
2. World declaration on the survival, protection and development of children. The challenge, the opportunity, the task, the commitment, the next steps, agreed to at the World Summit for children on September 30, 1990. New York: UNICEF; 1990. (See appendix B.)

Chapter 14. After the Summit for Children
1. Achieving health: New perspectives on integrated services and their contributions to mid-decade goals. Proceedings of the International Child Survival Conference, New Delhi, February 2-4, 1994. New York: The Rockefeller Foundation; 1994.
2. World Bank. World development report 1993: Investing in health. New York: Oxford University Press; 1993.

Chapter 17. The Task Force for Global Health
1. Rosenberg ML, Hayes ES, McIntyre MH, Neill N. Real collaboration: What it takes for global health to succeed. Berkeley: Milbank Memorial Fund and University of California Press; 2010.

2. An uneven recovery for America's biggest charities. News and Analysis. Chronicle of Philanthropy, October 20, 2013. The Philanthropy 400 was compiled by EC Grovum, S Frostenson, M Lopez-Rivera, and S Speicher.

Chapter 18. Lessons

1. The Millennium Development Goals, established following the Millennium Summit on the United Nations. New York: United Nations; 1990.
2. An uneven recovery for America's biggest charities. News and Analysis. Chronicle of Philanthropy, October 20, 2013. The Philanthropy 400 was compiled by EC Grovum, S Frostenson, M Lopez-Rivera, and S Speicher.
3. Bowles N. The Task Force for Child Survival—from 1984 through 1990. New York: UNICEF; 1991.

Appendix A

1. Heiser V. An American doctor's odyssey: Adventures in forty-five countries. New York: W. W. Norton; 1936.

INDEX

Page numbers in *italics* indicate graphs, illustrations, and photographs.

iodine, 56, 88
iron and anemia, 88
ivermectin. *See* Mectizan

jealousy over turf, 17-19
Jefferson, Thomas, 45
Jenner, Edward, 13
Johnson, Lyndon, 8
Joseph, Steve, 28, *29,* 31, 38, 41, 44

Keja, Ko, 16
Keynes, John Maynard, 101
Kim-Farley, Robert, 72
King, Stacey, 106, 107
Ko, U. Ko, 74
Kostrzewski, Jan, 27, *29*

Laney, Jim, 34-35
Langmuir, Alex, 2-3
LaPointe, Mark, 44
leadership, 94-95, 119, 121
Leschly, Jan, 110
lessons learned, 24-25, 39, 80, 118-23
Lincoln, Abraham, 95
Lloyd, John, 16
Lyman, Richard, 27, *29*
lymphatic filiariasis, 109-11, 114

Mahler, Halfdan: at Bellagio conference,
    27, *29;* Grant and, ix, 24; polio and,
    64; primary health care and, 18-19;
    Task Force and, ix, 3
Mashler, William, *29,* 38
Mason, Jim, 33
maternal health, 76
Maynard, Jim, 71
McGinnis, Mike, 66
McNamara, Robert, 22, 27, *29,* 31,
    43-44
McPherson, Peter, 27, *29*
Measham, Tony, 38
measles vaccine, 8, 9-11, 56
Mectizan: Donation Program, x, 5-6, 72,
    80-81, 99-102, 118; Expert Committee,
    3, 57, 102, 104, 109; relieves itching,
    103; safety of, 102-3

meningitis vaccine (MenAfriVac), 97
Merck & Co., x, 3, 5, 57, 110-11. *See also*
    Mectizan
micronutrients, 88-89
military, immunizations for, 10
Millar, J. D., 9
Miller, Rhena Schweitzer, 2
Moores, John, 105-6
Morse, Brad, 27, *29*
mumps vaccine, 8
Museveni, Yoweri, 55

Nakajima, Hiroshi, 64, 71-72, 78, 80, 84,
    87, 120
needle safety, 54
neonatal tetanus, 69-70
North, John, *29,* 38
Nossal, Gus, 27, *29,* 30

objectives of Task Force, 47-48
onchocerciasis, x, 3, 5, 57, 99-100.
    See also Mectizan
oral polio vaccine, 23, 81
Ottesen, Eric, 109

Pakistan, neonatal tetanus in, 69-70
Pan American Health Organization
    (PAHO), 10, 44, 47, 119
Paulson, Tom, 87
Pigman, Herb, 63
polio: eradication of, ix, 11, 63-64, 67,
    114; vaccines for, 7-8, 22, 23, 81, 103,
    111
politics and public health, 56, 72, 121
population growth rates, 61-63, *62*
primary health care, 17, 18, 64
problem solving, as function of coali-
    tions, 120-21
Program for Appropriate Technology in
    Health, 16

Quadros, Ciro de, 44, 47

Ramalingaswami, V., 27, *29*
Ravenholt, Rei, 2
representatives to Task Force, 37-39

INDEX   145

Watson, William, 33, 34, 39
Weller, Tom, 3
WHO. *See* World Health Organization
Wills, Garry, 95
WIN (*World Immunization News*) newsletter, 53
Wolfensohn, James, 93-94
World Bank, ix, 22, 38, 89-90, 93, 106
"World Declaration on the Survival, Protection and Development of Children," 85, 133-37
World Health Assembly, 8, 14, 64
World Health Organization (WHO): Alma-Ata program, 17, 64; applied research projects of, 54; coalition formation and, 22, 24-25; employees of, 15; immunization campaign of, 14; limitations of, 15, 118, 119; Onchocerciasis Control Program, 100; polio and, 23, 63-64; role of, 40; sculpture at, 106; UNICEF and, 42-43. *See also* Expanded Programme on Immunization; Mahler, Halfdan; Nakajima, Hiroshi; Task Force for Child Survival

Young, Andrew, 57, 95